Don't Shoot 'm: He's too Sick!

Billy's Story...One of Survival, Hope, and Miracles.

By Leah Price and Dr. Kay Linke

Table of Contents

Prologue 5

Chapter 1 - He Will Be Healed 7

Chapter 2 - Flash Back 9

Chapter 3 - Acts of Tenderness & Kindness 18

Chapter 4 - Friday the 13th 20

Chapter 5 - Twists of Fate or Miracles…You decide… 26

Chapter 6 - Dr. Linke's Perspective 30

Chapter 7 - Funny moments in the midst of sadness 40

Chapter 8 - The Doctor and The Diagnosis 43

Chapter 9 - The Roller Coaster 50

Chapter 10 - The downward spiral… 55

Chapter 11 - Is it time to stop? 60

Chapter 12 - God Provides 63

Chapter 13 - Angels, Angels, Everywhere 66

Chapter 14 - The Routine of Life & Death 73

Chapter 15 - Well, he is too sick to be here 78

Chapter 16 - Living in Crisis: 85

Chapter 17 - Spiritual Digression: 88

Chapter 18 - "Now Hope is for what we cannot see." 91

Chapter 19 - Can It Get Any Worse? 96

Chapter 20 - The Diagnosis 102

Chapter 21 - Prayer for Intervention – I didn't mean for anyone to get hurt 106

Chapter 22 - "Later" had arrived 108

Chapter 23 - Lucky Star 116

Chapter 24 - Good Luck 119

Chapter 25 - Treatment begins 126

Chapter 26 - Do or Die 130

Chapter 27 - What Else Can Happen? 135

Chapter 28 - Kidney Failure 139

Chapter 29 - The Calm before the Storm 142

Chapter 30 - What are we saving him for? 158

Chapter 31 - Letting Go and Giving it to God 170

Chapter 32 - On the Edge 177

Chapter 33 - Real and Sustained Progress 180

Chapter 34 - Patience 187

Chapter 35 - The Parade! 189

Chapter 36 - Plan B 197

Chapter 37 - Unusual but Happy Anniversary 203

Chapter 38 - Dom Perignon 205

Chapter 39 - Grow Old Along with Me 211

Epilogue – Perspectives 214

Prologue

Just over twenty-five years ago, my 34 year old husband of four and one-half years was suddenly diagnosed with a very aggressive stage four cancer and given no hope for recovery. He was so sick that the only course of action was to try to prolong his life if only for a few weeks. Many would ask, "Why treat him, he is too sick?"…in other words, "Save the bullet".

As the scripture says, "Now hope that is seen is not hope. For who hopes for what he sees?" (Romans 8:24) Come along on this journey and discover God's imminence especially in the midst of crises, His provision at just the right moments, living hope when there is no evidence for hope, the goodness of humanity, and miracles.

For anyone desiring proof of a higher power, practical steps to cope in crisis, how to "live" hope, and evidence of miracles, this story is for you.

Thank you to my family (Lu and Bill Price, Lou Walter, Lydia Lyon, Memaw Penry, Clyde Penry, and Herb Penry, friends (Tonda Shelton, David Skeels, Brad Penn, Mary Robinson, Kathy Brammer, Jim Melvin, and 1st Home Federal family, and countless others), and even strangers who were there for us on this journey, Dr. Linke for her competence and courage, and MD Anderson Cancer Center. Most of all, thank you God for miracles.

Copyright 6/23/17. In accordance with the U.S. Copyright Act of 1976, the scanning, uploading, and electronic sharing of any part of this book without the permission of the publisher constitute unlawful piracy and theft of the author's intellectual property.

Chapter 1 - He Will Be Healed...

September 17, 1991: Here we are on a plane headed to MD Anderson Cancer Center in Houston, TX, September 17th, 1991. Billy has an appointment at 9:00 on September 18th, 1991, my 33rd Birthday. I find myself reflecting over the events of the past week - how our lives have spiraled out of control as my husband, Billy, was diagnosed with a stage four cancer called sarcoma. Our local doctor told us that there was no treatment for sarcoma that had metastasized throughout the lungs as Billy's had. All he could do was try to find a teaching university somewhere across the country that had the most advanced trial studies for sarcomas, hence our current destination of Houston, TX.

As Billy sits, staring ahead in silence, there is only the hum of the engines, and his labored breathing as I think to myself, "Isn't it ironic that of all times, the appointment was scheduled on my Birthday." Then I think, "wouldn't it be the greatest gift in the world if Billy were healed for my birthday…Yes…yes it would"…when suddenly I hear this voice in my head say…"he will be healed", and then again…"he will be healed." A warm, tingling sensation flowed down my body, arms and fingers.

Chapter 2 - Flash Back

September 2, 1991...It was just over a week ago when Billy had been trimming his beard and putting on his deodorant when he told me about a knot that he had found under his arm. We had two eager and joyful Dalmatians who loved to walk their owners, so a pulled muscle was the likely explanation. Now, I remember wondering whether a pulled muscle could cause a knot like that, but at that moment it seemed to be a reasonable conclusion. For the past several months Billy had seemed overly fatigued for a 34-year-old man. He had developed a nagging cough which the doctors had been treating as an allergy. I had been urging him to see a doctor again because this fatigue didn't seem normal.

September 5: Billy finally went to see the doctor. When he returned home, I was anxious to know what the doctors thought could be causing his fatigue and cough. He said that the doctors did not comment about that. In a strangely somber tone, he said that they were actually more intrigued about the knot. I had not given the knot a second thought since Monday because he had not complained about it further. I wanted to press him about the other issues but something in his voice stopped me.

September 6: The next day Billy called me from home to tell me that he had started having chills. The doctors had prescribed some antibiotics with the idea that the knot was some sort of staph or strep infection. He decided to stay home.

September 7: Saturday night we were having a Labor Day celebration. Billy laid around most of the day while I was cleaning. Billy never complained much and this was no exception, but I could tell that he did not feel well because he wasn't joking around with me like he always did. When our friends arrived, we set up our new cheap volleyball set in the backyard and proceeded with some heated matches. Billy just watched quietly and kept score which again was very "un-Billy-like". He was always in the middle of anything fun. When we came inside to watch our feature movie, "Misery", Billy went to bed. It was only around 8:00. I checked on him every few minutes. He had chills. He was very quiet.

September 8: Sunday morning, Billy's ribs were hurting and the chills persisted. He seemed unusually concerned. I got a thermometer from my sister, Lou, who lived in a house across the street. He had a slight fever. Having been on antibiotics since Thursday, he should have been getting better, I thought. The knot under his arm was bigger. I called Billy's mother, Lu, who worked at a doctor's office. She suggested that I take Billy to the emergency room where Dr. Rowe, one of the doctors at her practice, would be on call.

I took him to the ER. I could sense that Billy was scared. Since we had been married, Billy had never been sick so I did not know how he reacted under these circumstances.

Dr. Rowe took him back for what seemed like FOR-EVER. Finally, Dr. Rowe came out to speak with me. He told me that they were drawing fluid from the knot and checking for all kinds of things including the Plague. He rolled his eyes and said that he could not believe that it was the Plague.

"That would be bizarre but infectious disease people think of everything", he said with sarcasm. The doctor still thought it was a staph or strep infection. He said that I could go back and see Billy now. I found him in the exam room. His typically little squinty eyes looked big. He had a baseball cap on. There were tears in his eyes. He almost seemed childlike. I wanted to comfort him. I held his hand and hugged him. He told me that they had been poking at his knot as if he was tattling on the doctors. He motioned with his hands as he described the size of the huge needle that they stuck in it. "They drew fluid out, and it hurt so badly", he said, as his lip quivered.

The initial tests were inconclusive so Dr. Rowe decided to admit him. I didn't want to leave him at the hospital, so I stayed with him that night. That night his fever climbed to 102.

September 9: I decided to stay with him the next day too. I never missed work and it did not seem critical at that point but I did not want to leave him in the face of uncertainty. Monday night his fever reached 103.

September 10: Tuesday night his temperature crept up to 104. The intravenous antibiotics should have been working by then. This was a really tough staph or strep, the doctors surmised.

September 11: On Wednesday, he developed this awful, wheezing cough – kind of dry but with a croupy whistle. My sister, Lydia who is a nurse, was staying with me at the hospital at this point and kept insisting that they culture his sputum, but no one seemed interested. The doctors started talking about surgery to remove the infectious area to provide some relief if there was no improvement. Wednesday night his fever spiked to 105 and the cough worsened to a dry whistle. Lydia slept in a recliner on the side of the bed, periodically packing him in ice and reorienting him as to where he was. He couldn't sleep because he coughed with every other breath. He would groan and began to get disoriented throughout the night. The nurses would bring him cough medicine that must have tasted lemony. Billy loved it. At one point, he stretched out his hand in a sweeping motion across to Lydia and me and asked the nurse to bring a couple of cases for his "monterage" along with some double beds. Then he started talking about the chocolate that was dripping from the ceiling. When I insisted that there really wasn't any chocolate there, he got really agitated so I decided to slide into the bed next to him and started to describe how rich and delicious it looked as it dropped from the ceiling. The nights were so long and seemed like an eternity.

When they first mentioned surgery, Billy was insistent against it. By Thursday morning, he wanted them to get the knot out of him. He had suffered so much. For some reason, the surgery was delayed from early Thursday until noon. Billy was dreading it terribly. My sister, Lydia, mom, and Billy's mom, Lu, and dad, Bill – all lined the hallway as they wheeled Billy out for surgery. They did not give him any pre-op sedation and Billy was especially nervous. I walked alongside the gurney to the elevator, telling him I loved him, and that he would feel much better when he woke up. I was trying to be strong, but tears were welling up and I could hear my voice shaking. As the doors closed, we all turned to walk down to the waiting room.

It was 1:20. I wondered why it was taking so long. It had been 80 minutes. Everyone was joking nervously just trying to pass the time, when the doctor came to the door. We all scurried over and encircled him in the doorway to the waiting room where 15-20 people were sitting. He hesitated momentarily and then said, "Well folks...it looks like we've got a malignancy here." I remember everyone gasping and then he continued to speak although I was not making out a word that he was saying. At that moment, nothing seemed to matter for all that I knew about cancer, which wasn't much, it was all over. Cancer, no, not Billy, I thought. They must be wrong. No. All I could see in my mind was bald heads, deteriorating bodies, and hallowed faces. I am not strong enough for this. They took us to another room. Everyone was crying. I ran out. I thought if I ran, I could escape the reality of what was happening. Outside where the sky was big, I could get some air and wake up from this nightmare. I found myself in the park outside the hospital calling out for God. Where was He? I did not feel His presence. Not that I questioned why this was happening to Billy and me. Why not? But what was I going to do? What does one do when the rug of life is suddenly ripped out from under one's feet?

I returned inside, but I couldn't quit crying. How was Billy going to feel when they broke him the news? They did not want to tell him until the "oncologist" – just one of the many new medical terms I was to learn over the next several months – came to visit Billy that night. I was supposed to go back into Billy's room when he awakened from surgery and not let on about anything…yeah right …no problem. Sure, he wouldn't notice that my eyes were almost swollen shut and that I heaved a sob with every other breath. The thought of me knowing this dreadful diagnosis and him not knowing anything was unbearable. Shortly, more of our family and the ministers were gathered in the hallway outside his door. Someone was telling me that Billy was looking for me. They said he was going to wonder why I was not in there. Okay…I thought I've got to take a deep breath and go in. I have got to be strong for him. After taking one more deep breath, I slowly walked in. "Hey Billy", I said with a half-smile, voice quivering, and tears spilling over the brims of my eyes. His eyes lit up when he saw me and he said, "Hey baby...I feel much better now...I think".

The doctor finally came by and shared the news with Billy. Among other things he told us that the lymph node was encapsulated so maybe it had not metastasized – spread though his body...another new medical term. If it had not metastasized it would be considered a Stage 1. There were, basically, four stages with Stage 4 meaning that it had spread to multiple organs. They would conduct a CT scan tomorrow to stage the disease.

Chapter 3 - Acts of Tenderness & Kindness:

My soul ached to the core with a sadness, fear, and despair that I had never felt before. There were to be many moments when family, friends, and even strangers unexpectedly performed acts of tenderness and kindness that lifted my soul in the darkest and bleakest moments, when knowing that God was still there was vital. I was not aware at the time how God was using these moments to carry me through. My awareness came later after so many of these moments transpired that the significance and pattern was revealed.

One of those sweet moments came when my nephew, Josh, fifteen at the time, had his dad, Ken, bring him to the hospital the day of the diagnosis to see me. I will never forget how this young man that lacked the time for life experiences to teach him compassion took me by the shoulders, looked deep into my eyes, and asked, "Are you ok?" The sincere concern and love was clearly etched on his face. This simple act lifted my heart. I saw God's compassion in his eyes.

Later the evening of the same day, I realized that I had not eaten all day. I wasn't hungry but knew that I needed to eat. I ventured downstairs to the café and took a chocolate chip cookie from the basket. The guy behind the counter must have seen my puffy eyes and the sorrow and despair on my face. With pain in his eyes he said, "Just take it- you look like you really need it." A total stranger shared my pain. Once again, though small, this sincere act of kindness was reminding me that God was all around me.

There were countless other moments like these to be experienced over the upcoming months, when God revealed his tender love to me that I may have never seen had it **not been for the life and death reality of the circumstances.**

Chapter 4 - Friday the 13th

September 13th: It seemed eerily ironic and unnerving as we waited on what I envisioned in my mind as Dr. Death in a black cloak to deliver the results of the CT scan on Friday the 13th of all days. We were sitting anxiously awaiting the oncologist's visit to find out about Billy's prognosis. When he finally arrived late that evening, we learned that the cancer had spread throughout his lungs and the cough that was worsening was most definitely related. Billy asked if they could do surgery to remove it and the doctor replied, "oh no, it has spread so much that surgery is not an option". Then is when he told us that he would need to search for a university across the country that specialized in treating sarcomas. It is such a rare cancer there had not been much success in its treatment once it had metastasized. We would need to go somewhere that specialized in this type of cancer because we needed to be aggressive with the treatment. There were so many times over the weeks to come where Billy's reaction to our dire circumstances would blow me away. The first was when the doctor left the room and Billy turned to me and said, "Ain't that some shit? Doesn't sound like good news to me." Then tears came in his eyes. I assumed that his statement was in reaction to the prognosis when he asked, "How are you with the situation? This means that you won't be able to be with me", I realized his concerns were for me and having me with him. I said, oh no Billy, I will be with you wherever you go, don't worry about that.

September 14th: My sister, Lydia, asked the doctor if they were treating Billy for an infection because his cough continued to worsen. They said, "Oh no, they were not going to treat him for infection because the cough was related to the cancer. Billy did not have an infection." They began some steroids to mask the fever symptoms in order to provide some relief to enable him for air travel. The doctor obviously felt great urgency in securing the referral to cancer center as soon as possible as Billy's condition was deteriorating so rapidly.

Later, friends began to hear about Billy's condition and started to gather in a line outside his door at the hospital. A steady stream of our friends took turns coming into his room to visit for short periods. It was during this time that Billy looked over at me and said, "We are the lucky ones. We have the bird's eye seat and get to sit here all the time while everyone else has to take turns to come in here to see us." Interestingly, I had not seen the joy in this moment as he had. What a unique perspective.

Billy never once complained or asked why. He faced his illness with the same optimism that he did in all other aspects of life.

September 15th: At 5:00 a.m. Billy got dressed and said he was ready to go home. He sat in the chair waiting for the doctor. When the doctor arrived, Billy begged him to let him go home. It was as if he wanted to get out and find some normalcy. After several pleas for parole, the doctor finally, reluctantly, relented and gave him a pass for the day with the agreement he would return by night. For some reason, this day passed as if it were in slow motion. It is funny how every moment counts when you are intently aware that the remaining moments are very limited. Billy asked me if I wanted to go by the service station that we frequented for years, hang out with the boys, and flaunt my stuff because I had been winning in the football pool that we shared the last couple of weeks. Now the simplest things like this seemed so precious. Afterwards we spent a little time at home with the dogs and it was time to head back to the hospital.

September 16th: Billy was discharged and we headed home. Most of the day was just spent getting ready to leave as we had been told that we would be headed to MD Anderson Cancer Center in Houston Texas the next day. (I learned later that it was amazing that we had been able to get an appointment so quickly.) At one point, I was sitting on the floor beside the couch as he lay resting. It is then that he told me that he was glad that we had good insurance. Even though he knew that it would not take his place, he wanted me to use it to give me some temporary pleasure and to relieve the pain. He asked that I not let others' expectations dictate my grief. Some people would frown if I seemed to go on without him too soon. Amazing, he was not thinking of himself and his circumstances but was only thinking of me and my future. Wow...would I be that composed, unselfish and accepting of such a sudden and certain end to my life...I would hope so, but think not.

September 16th: I went back into work briefly on Monday to tie up loose ends. I remember a card that my co-worker, Mary, gave to me. In it she said that she prayed that God would go before us and prepare a place – a path. It was so comforting to think that God would go ahead and make ready for us, especially when the future and the path seemed so uncertain and out of control.

September 17th: Billy, his mom, Lu, and I board the plane headed toward Houston. We were told that it would be just a couple of days because they would be conducting an assessment and determining the appropriate protocol for the presentment of his disease. Treatments would be administered locally so we had packed lightly. This is when I received the divine message that Billy would be healed that I referenced previously. How could I be smiling...there was absolutely no evidence to support hope? By nature, I am an optimist but I am a realist too. We had been given no reason for hope, and yet I heard this message and felt this deep assurance that God was in our midst and in control of this unimaginable ordeal.

Chapter 5 - Twists of Fate or Miracles...You decide...

Throughout this ordeal, there were numerous occasions where had circumstances been different - at times by minutes - Billy would have died. Again, as with the tender moments, the pattern and trend of these events was not obvious until with time, reflection, and the accumulation of incidences, it became obvious that there was a greater power in control orchestrating these events.

The first of these occurrences happened when the doctors gave Billy the medicine that helped to mask his infectious symptoms. After the diagnosis on Friday, September 12, the doctor quickly worked to identify a teaching hospital with trials for treating this rare cancer. Normally it can take weeks, but we were on our way to Houston in 5 days. As we arrived at the hotel, Billy's infectious symptoms started to return rapidly. Clearly, if we had been delayed even by one day, Billy's condition would have rendered him ineligible for travel to Houston where the hope that was given was that his life may be extended if only for a short while.

His mother and I were up all night trying to comfort Billy, packing him in ice, as he suffered and ached with fever and chills. By the morning, we were on a mission just to make it to the appointment. When I awakened him, Billy said he was sorry but he didn't feel like he could shower and that he would have to go dirty, like that really mattered at this point. I took my first cab ride as we maneuvered through the maze of the MD Anderson complex - which I was to later appreciate was one of the largest and internationally renowned cancer centers in the world - to the lobby of the clinic where we sat on the floor so that I could cradle Billy's head in my hands trying to hold out just a few more minutes when I could entrust his care into the hands of one much more capable than me.

MD Anderson, I would learn, treated hundreds of thousands of patients yearly from all over the world. Houston was one of the largest cities in the country with a population in excess of 6 million at the time. I had not ventured much further than North Carolina's borders. Life at this moment had travelled so far beyond the limits of my imagination but I did not have time to contemplate on how overwhelming the reality of our situation had become.

Nine o'clock finally arrived and Billy's name is called. It is impossible to express what a relief it was to relinquish the immediate responsibility of Billy's care. We were taken back to an office where the nurse began to assess him. I could tell she was surprised at the acute nature of his symptoms. She left and another person enters who, I learn later is a "fellow" and continues the assessment. ("Fellow" - another medical term which I learned was the period of medical training that a physician may undertake after completing a specialty training program). Dr. Linke follows. She is "THE" doctor specialized in sarcoma that is assigned to this case. I am sitting on the table beside Billy wanting desperately for any words of hope. "Help" I yelled silently. She was obviously young but exudes an air of competence and confidence. I was encouraged that she would be the one to provide answers. After her own assessments she said, "I am not saying that he does not have cancer, but there is something else going on," and told us that she was admitting him for further treatment.

Chapter 6 - Dr. Linke's Perspective

September 12, 1991: I sat at my office desk working on my research project and studying for Medical Oncology Boards. I had decided to stay on staff after completing the 3-year Fellowship in Medical Oncology to help finish a research project that was quite extensive. I had hoped in about 6 more months I would finish this project and move back to Ohio to go into private practice. For a recent addition to the medical staff at MD Anderson, I was fortunate to have an office with a window. Of course, the window only offered a view of the loading dock. My research project was the accumulation of at least 30 years of patients treated at University of Texas, M. D. Anderson Cancer Center with the diagnosis of soft tissue sarcoma. Soft tissue sarcomas are a wide variety of tumors that grow in the support structures of the body such as muscles, tendons and ligaments. The aggressive ones spread to the lungs which is quite problematic in their care and reduces the chance of long term remission.

Hopefully, the database would help us learn about what worked best for these malignancies and what didn't. I had spent over a year locating information on these patients that had been treated at this rapidly expanding institution. When I was not in the clinic seeing patients, my days were absorbed in reviewing patient charts, some of which were so old they had to be brought out of storage and read on a microfiche document reader. I copied path reports and logged tumor sizes and original sites of the sarcoma. I looked for treatments done with dates of surgeries, extent of radiation treatment, and dates and doses of chemotherapy. I looked for second surgeries to see if the tumor had regressed and if it was completely removed. Dates of recurrences and sites of recurrences were recorded, as well with more treatment information. Other days were spent making follow up calls to patients to see if further events had occurred and how they were doing. Some patients would remain lost to follow up, but one gentleman claimed he would never return to Houston. He related that MD Anderson did a great job on his sarcoma, which remained in remission. He suffered a fall on his last visit to MD Anderson when leaving the building and had to be brought in for surgery on his fractured hip.

All this information was being placed in an electronic data base that would help bring into focus as to what type of tumors needed more extensive treatment and perhaps would offer clues to what treatment plans offered the best options of care and outcomes. No matter how many times I looked at this information and kept meticulous records, there seemed to be some inconsistencies in the data base and it was my job to make sure the information was as accurate as possible.

The phone rang. It was the Physician Referral Service who said a Doctor from North Carolina was on the line to refer a newly diagnosed sarcoma patient. The doctor, with a soft Southern accent, described a young man that was recently found to have a mass under the left arm. The limited biopsy of this mass was called a malignant sarcoma by their pathologist, but they couldn't classify it any further. He wondered if we could offer advice on his treatment options, if the patient came to Houston. I responded that we would be happy to see this patient and the Physician Referral person took over to help arrange for an appointment at our clinic in Houston, Texas.

The Department of Melanoma and sarcoma included nine physicians that could treat patients with these diagnoses. Six physicians of our department were able to treat patients with sarcomas, so it was possible I wouldn't see the patient who was just referred when he arrived. A sarcoma found under the arm seemed odd to me. Most of the sarcomas of the arm area would be in the muscles like the biceps or triceps or on the shoulder, rather than under the arm. Perhaps the referring physician used the wrong term to describe the location.

I went back to reviewing the data base information. At the time, I was unaware that phone call concerning the patient in North

Carolina would dramatically change my next 6 months.

September 18: It was just about 9 am and I had finished rounding on patients in the hospital and was sitting at my desk working on dictating notes when the nurse covering my clinic came in. She was not my usual clinic nurse and her question was quite intriguing. She asked, "Will you be admitting your new patient today?" I had not seen the patient yet and didn't know anything about him, not even his name. She gave no further information. Admitting sarcoma patients to the hospital on a first visit is really quite rare. New patients usually are early in the workup process and need more tests before any treatment would be initiated. Although sarcoma patients would be in the hospital for treatment with chemotherapy or for treatment of chemotherapy complications such as infection, admission would be unlikely on a first visit.

"Why do you ask? I replied.

"He is very ill. There is a Fellow in with him now." She stated.

"I will be in to see him soon" I answered.

I went back to my dictations and a few minutes later the Fellow came in and sat down in the chair across from my desk. "Do you think you will admit your new patient today?" he asked. He had some papers in his hands and a note sheet.

"I have a feeling I am since you are the second person to ask that. What do you know about this new patient so far?" I requested.

The Fellow explained that this 34-year-old man from North Carolina presented with a lump in the left armpit that he found while showering and was sent for a biopsy of the mass. He had related that the patient had about one year of worsening fatigue prior to finding the lump. He was admitted to the hospital and found to have worsening fevers and an increasing cough. He was started on antibiotics and physicians felt that the lump was infected. Testing on the lungs was done with a CT scan showed a mass in the left armpit area and concern over involvement with infiltrates in the both lung bases. The comment about the mass under the arm crossed my mind. A biopsy was done and it showed a very aggressive malignant sarcoma and he was referred at that point to MD Anderson   Now I knew it related back to the phone call I had received last week.

The Fellow went on to explain that despite the antibiotics, his fever didn't subside. They started more antibiotics and more extensive look for infectious causes offered nothing new. He was then placed on prednisone to see if that would lower the fevers and it did. The patient did improve and was released, so he could travel to Houston.

He arrives in my clinic for further evaluation and apparently based on both the Nurse's and the Fellow's evaluation was sick enough to be admitted today. The Fellow related that he was lying on the floor of the waiting room when they went to get him to place him the exam room. It would be extremely rare for a malignant sarcoma under the arm to make someone so ill, so early in the presentation. Also, out of the ordinary were the fevers. It didn't fit a picture of sarcoma very well at this point, in my opinion.

I asked the fellow what tests or radiographs had been brought along to review and he stated they brought some chart records, x-rays, and the pathology slides. Those were good places to start to put this complex case together.

We went to the conference room where we could look at the X-rays. A Chest CT Scan showed a mass in the left armpit and some enlarged lymph nodes in the middle of the chest, between the lungs. He also appeared to have some pneumonia process in both lungs. The Fellow and I discussed his situation briefly and decided he was ill enough to be admitted. With the lowering of the dose of prednisone his fevers were worsening and his breathing was worsening. We grabbed the package of slides and decided to get the admission process started.

I went into the clinical exam room and the patient, Billy Price was lying on the exam table. He was as pale as the white sheet that covered him and his breathing was rapid and shallow. His wife, Leah Price, sat with her knees tucked up under her chin and with brown eyes as large as saucers. I was aware of another older woman was sitting in the corner by the door. I went to talk to Billy and related that I wasn't sure what he had at this time, but I was sure he needed to be back in the hospital to figure it out. I felt for sure we had an infectious process to treat. I also related that there was a cancer process we would need to work on, but was unclear if this was truly a sarcoma. I told him our Pulmonary Service and Infectious Disease Service would see him as I was sure he had a process in the lungs that needed further examination and care. I knew that we needed to think broader in terms of diagnoses here as the picture didn't fit a soft tissue sarcoma very well, and other diagnoses were possible. I excused myself stating we were heading to Pathology department to see what information they might be able to offer from the pathology slides. I related that I would stop by later to their room to follow up on his case.

We talked to the office staff and let them know to arrange for a hospital bed and we wrote some basic admission orders which included some x-rays, blood cultures, antibiotics, and consultations with Pulmonary and Infectious Disease Physicians.

The Fellow and I grabbed the biopsy slides and went down the back stairs to Pathology Department.

Chapter 7 - Funny moments in the midst of sadness

September 18: After Dr. Linke left, we waited in the exam room. Her observations that there may be other causes for Billy's extreme symptoms gave me hope. Back home they would not even consider that there might be an infection. They were adamant that all of the symptoms were due to the cancer. Billy was taken to the ER. All kinds of tests were conducted and antibiotics were administered once again.

During some of the most difficult and overwhelmingly morbid situations, there would be funny things that would happen. At first, I couldn't understand and I felt guilty being able to laugh while Billy's life was in the balance, but I discovered that the new depths of pain that I was experiencing under these circumstances were matched with new depths in all emotions – sadness, humor and joy. Everything and every moment was so much more important because time was more sacred now. Each moment was life and death.

September 19th: One of those surprisingly funny moments occurred during Billy's bronchoscopy the next day. Billy, who was in pain and feverish as we waited for the test to be conducted, began to muffle sounds under his oxygen mask. Lu and I were so absorbed in the gravity of the moment that we did not initially notice the radio in the background playing Polk Salad Annie. Suddenly we realized that Billy was singing every word including the "chomp, chomp" and patting his feet.

September 18th – 21st: Billy continued to have high fevers. I stayed in the room around the clock. I wore my new Dalmatian shirt that was given to me for my birthday for 4 straight days, taking baths in the hospital bathroom. His mother and I shared a fold out chair in Billy's room. In describing the chair to a friend over the phone, Lu suggested it was the size of a pencil. During this time, I would constantly pack Billy in ice and feed him water. He was so sick that he did not have the strength to communicate. In the midst of this, one time he said, "I love you, Leah". I remember the sheer joy that I felt from knowing that he was still with me and fighting for his life because it was so lonely and scary fighting alone. They continued to perform tests trying to assess his disease and determine the source of infection. After the bronchoscopy, he kept fighting the oxygen mask and pulling it off. Lu and I kept putting it back on. At one point, he looked at us and said, "I'll get you two for this." Nothing could get his spirits down. He tried to convince me he couldn't wear the mask because of the x-ray they were getting ready to perform. When I asked the nurse on the way to the x-ray room if what Billy was saying was true, she said that Billy was fooling me. It tickled me to think that even in his sickness he still had his wicked humor.

Chapter 8 - The Doctor and The Diagnosis

After writing admission orders, my first goal was to review the available pathology slides. In Pathology, I asked if Dr. Evans, who was an expert in soft tissue sarcomas, was available. Luckily, he was and we went into his office and I asked him to see what he could tell us about the biopsy material obtained from under the left arm. He looked at the material and related it wasn't preserved very well and that might make a complete diagnosis problematic. That is a pathologist's way of saying another biopsy might be needed. I asked if he thought this could be a sarcoma to which he replied it was possible. His further description led me to believe he had no idea what tissue this tumor arrived from or started in. I asked if he thought this could be other cancers too and he related that any cancer was possible with this tissue, "Any malignancy?" The diagnosis list expanded exponentially now. Did he include carcinomas to that list? He replied any cancer was possible. Did he include melanoma in that list of possibilities? He related melanoma was also possible. Did he consider sarcomas on the list of possible causes? He replied yes. Certainly, a more extensive look at further risk factors and past medical history would be needed. I asked if there was anything that was not on the list of possibilities. He replied, "This is not Kaposi's Sarcoma." Could he exclude other possible answers?? He related that was the only one he could exclude at this time. Of all the possible cancers, only ONE was excluded.

The exclusion of Kaposi's Sarcoma was not insignificant for a young man with pneumonia and fevers. This presentation certainly could be seen in patients with HIV and our knowledge of those at risk was expanding throughout the prior decade that brought HIV and AIDS to the forefront of medical care and a national HIV scare. The picture certainly could have been that of full blown AIDS and to exclude "Kaposi's" Sarcoma was in fact a bit of relief, although, Kaposi's Sarcoma is not the only cancer seen in HIV patients.

With the possibility of HIV related malignancy being less, I was a bit relieved. While we would still check for HIV, as other malignancies can be seen in those patients, the rest of the malignancies still being possible looked quite daunting.

Arriving back at the clinic, we found that Billy Price had been moved to the hospital. I asked the Fellow to go check on him as I proceeded with other patients in the clinic. He came back and reported that both the Infectious Disease and Pulmonary Doctors were seeing Billy Price when he arrived. We proceeded with the daily clinic list. I had hoped to get back to seeing Billy soon to see what the consulting physicians thought about his case and to ask more questions that might clarify this situation and narrow down the malignancies that might be possible.

Later in the afternoon, I went up to the room with a list of questions to ask. I had found out that the infectious disease service had expanded the antibiotic coverage and started plenty of testing to look for rarer forms of infection such as Legionnaire's disease and other atypical forms of pneumonia, such as pneumocystis carinii. The Pulmonary Doctor was planning a bronchoscope, testing to look at the lung airways directly to help evaluate the pneumonia the next morning. I made sure that his medication orders included some prednisone, since it did seem that helped him briefly and it couldn't be stopped abruptly without making him feel far worse. Maybe he felt worse with the reduction of the steroid dose he had already encountered.

I went to see Billy and his breathing had worsened. He was breathing faster now, even with the addition of oxygen via a face mask. He was presently on 40% oxygen level via the mask, which is twice the amount in the air we breathe. He had spiked a fever to 102 degrees already and was having shaking rigors with them. This told me there had to be an infection involved here in this case.

I asked several questions that related to his personal life. He was married, but no children. He worked with leather goods, but the leather was already processed so he didn't touch raw animal skins. He related that they had just built a house and he did help in the digging of the wells, which exposed him to the soil in North Carolina. A Fungal infection could be possible with that information. He was in the Wesley Long hospital about a week before he came here. I wonder if he caught something there, but his wife related the fevers had started before he arrived at the hospital. Hospitals are notorious for having plenty of bacteria that can make the patients ill. He drank socially and was not a smoker. His only medical condition was hypertension that was treated with medication for several years. Family history revealed heart disease and hypertension. He denied any other issues and denied in particular any skin lesions that were removed to help rule out the possibility of this being related to a melanoma. Other than feeling melanoma would be less likely, the list of possible cancers remained quite lengthy.

His physical exam however was quite revealing. Along with his obvious breathing issues, he has some lumps along the left collar bone area. There were some enlarged lymph nodes or masses in the left armpit area, but less extensive than what was seen on the CT scan. Was that a biopsy effect or a prednisone effect? No other abnormalities were found, although Billy was quite weak and pale and worn out from the trip to Houston. He, his wife and Mother had flown to Houston the day before. The wife related that with the lowering dose of the prednisone, he became quite worse again. She did feel that the Prednisone offered him some improvement at the higher dose.

My thoughts at that time seemed to focus on the possibility that this was a lymphoma in the left armpit with further lymph nodes leading to the chest and up to the neck area. There was no evidence of any masses in the lungs or the partial view of the liver or spleen seen on the CT-Scan they sent along. The pneumonia could be almost any infection but an atypical form would need to be kept in mind. I went to the chart to check the list of antibiotics again. I wanted to make sure erythromycin was part of the treatment since that would help most of the atypical forms of pneumonia, such as Legionnaire's disease.

I talked to Dr. Evans at our afternoon meeting where our service reviewed new cases and he related he had no further help to offer from the pathology slides. The list of possible cancers remained wide open. I reported he was having a bronchoscope in the morning, so more material might be available from that.

It is no wonder the Clinic Nurse and the Fellow thought he should be admitted. Now, I worried that he may not have been admitted in time.

Chapter 9 - The Roller Coaster

Dr. Linke, Billy's physician, had left for a week-long trip on Friday, 9/20. I found out later it was for her Board Review. She had just finished her Fellowship in July. Intending to return to her home state to practice oncology, she decided in August to accept a position on staff at M.D. Anderson. With one month difference in the timing of Dr. Linke's completion of her training and a change in her choice just one month prior to our trip, Dr. Linke would not have been the attending physician, both factors of which we would learn later were critical for the aggressive treatment of his disease which was required.

September 21st: In the wee hours of Saturday morning, Billy's condition was worsening rapidly. He started to fade and become unresponsive. I kept packing him in ice as he felt so hot. It was all that I knew to do. It was what Lydia had done back home. I kept going out to the nurse's station pleading with someone to come in and check on Billy. I will never forget how the nurse with the huge bun kept telling me, "there is nothing we can do, Hun". She wouldn't even look at me. At the time, I could not understand why or how she could be so indifferent. With time, I grew to understand how that can happen when working in a cancer center. It becomes easy to assume that death is inevitable and that all symptoms are due to cancer; and, therefore, not react with urgency when other treatable conditions present an emergency. I felt alone and helpless seeing Billy's life fading away and feeling totally inadequate to help him. It was at this time as I was standing by Billy's bed that morning that he looked up at me and asked, "Where is everybody? Where are all of the doctors and nurses?" He knew he was going down-hill fast and was ready for an all-out effort. He said, "Don't leave me, Leah…keep checking on me."

It was at the shift change that an Intern came in to check Billy's vital signs. He found his blood pressure at 70/50 and that Billy was in "septic shock". In other words, his organs were shutting down. He looked at me incredulously and asked me how long he had been like this and told me that we needed to get him in ICU ASAP! He was dying. Finally, a clutter of motion started to happen as the staff prepared Billy for transport to

ICU. I experienced relief as again I could transfer the responsibility of keeping Billy on this side of eternity to others. We were told to go to the ICU waiting room and wait for someone after they attempted to stabilize and assess Billy's condition. This is another one of the instances where had this nurse not intervened at this precise moment, Billy would have died.

After a couple of hours of nervous pacing and minds racing about what was happening, the attending ICU physician came in to inform us that Billy's condition was grave. His organs were shutting down. They were pumping him with high dosages of steroids and antibiotics, hoping to stabilize his condition. The next 24 hours were critical as they waited to see if his body would respond and rebound. It would be a roller coaster ride. All we could do was wait and see. I cried hysterically as the gravity of the situation was overwhelming. Life was spinning out of control. It had gone from bad to worse. There was nothing we could do but wait. The doctor said that once they got Billy stabilized they would let us go back to see with him before he was intubated.

In the ICU in the midst of this near-death moment, Billy looked at me and said, "This shit better work." He rolled his eyes and curled his lip and said, "They catharized me", and then he asked, "Are my goodies showing?" He had been in ER, 9th, 8th floors, and now in ICU in only a matter of three days. Apparently, aware of this, he was ready to go again as he asked, "What room now girls?" Amazingly...we laughed in the face of death.

During the first days that Billy was in ICU, most of our time was spent in the waiting room as we were limited to 30 minute visits 4 times per day. Billy's condition was so precarious that we could not leave. Just outside of the ICU waiting room, there was a small bathroom probably no bigger than three feet by three feet. Having been days since having access to a bathroom, I was desperate for a bath so I decided to try to wash my hair in this small water closet. Shortly after getting my head underneath the faucet I realized it was wedged so tight that I couldn't get it out. I panicked. My back was facing the door so I contemplated kicking backwards to call for help. Before executing this plan, I tried to relax telling myself that if I was able to get it under there I should be able to pry my head loose. Thankfully, once I calmed down I was able to get free.

At 10:00 each night, the staff would bring pillows and blankets for families who were staying around the clock in the ICU waiting room. Lu snores loudly, so much that one time she told a lady who sat down beside her that she may want to sit somewhere else. The lady responded that she had a solution and went on to describe how if Lu started to snore all she had to do was lift Lu's arm and gently drop it. Lu said she immediately got up and moved because she knew that the lady was going to break her arm. A couple of days later the Patient Care Coordinator, who will go unnamed, approached me to say that Lu could not sleep in the ICU waiting room any longer because of her snoring. What would we do? I did not want to be by myself. I told her that if Lu could not stay that I would not either. To which she responded "you cannot leave because you have to be here to sign for the body".

Chapter 10 - The downward spiral...

September 19 and Sept. 20, 1991: After admitting Billy Price from clinic, the next few days seemed to be more of the same for Billy with worsening issues. His breathing continued to deteriorate and his need for more oxygen supplementation rose. He was now on 60% oxygen and looked more uncomfortable by the day. The Pulmonologist that did the bronchoscope told me that he did not see anything abnormal in the airways. He showed me pictures of the airways that to my untrained eye looked very normal. That did not surprise me, but I hoped the material he had obtained by aspiration of lung fluids or biopsy, might find the cause of the pneumonia. Actually, I hoped we were treating it already with the antibiotics being given. His fevers continued twice daily to at least 104 degrees and at times higher. The fevers were accompanied by shaking chills and worsening mental status. He became confused during these events although seemed to be better when his temperature was more normal. His blood counts and liver and kidney tests by blood were normal at this time, but he was severely pale. His Chest X-ray was showing progression of the pneumonia process in both lungs.

At the close of Friday afternoon clinic, I knew Billy was not in good shape. I felt we had done all we could have done within the last 3 days to help make a difference in his care. I had to go home to pack for a trip to Boston. Medical Oncology Boards were coming up and I was to go to the Harvard Medical Oncology Board Review in the morning. I was leaving Billy in the hands of the other physicians in my department. We had talked over the last couple days about his case and they were well aware of his deteriorating condition, my concern for him to have pneumonia, but also a malignancy, and felt overall a lymphoma was the most likely diagnosis. I felt confident they would do their best to help Billy Price while I was gone for the week.

As I was packing up the car on Saturday morning, my pager beeped. It was a nurse on the floor where Billy was admitted. He advised me of his concern for the dropping blood pressure and increased labored breathing. I related that another doctor was covering but we would need to transfer him to the Intensive Care Unit as soon as possible. I ordered some IV fluids to help support his blood pressure, increased the oxygen level on his mask to the highest level possible, and made sure his blood pressure medication was held. I called the covering physician to alert him to the situation and to expect further calls on his situation. We would try to do everything possible for such a young man, who became so rapidly ill.

I hopped in the car. What would Billy be like in a week? Would he still be alive in a week? The Pulmonary service was still stumped. The Infectious Disease service felt they were using the best antibiotics available. The prednisone was still on board. But Billy's overall condition was heading in the wrong direction. The question remained about the type of malignancy he clearly had and also how advanced it was. How much more could his body handle? I hoped he could tolerate more considering his young age and the fact he was healthy until about 3 weeks ago. Of course, we have all seen those patients that became too sick to help in time. These types of presentations are the most gut-wrenching situations we deal with in medicine.

The next week while I was getting ready for Medical Oncology Boards at the hands of Harvard Medical School's Physicians, I took time to call in to the office in Houston. Dr. Patel related to me that Billy was now on full ventilator support and his lung condition was still worsening. He related his blood pressure had dropped drastically but with removing his blood pressure medication and adding in some fluids his blood pressure was now stable and back to a normal range. He also said that the testing from the bronchoscope showed the possible diagnosis of Legionnaire's disease. He said that the Infectious Disease and Pulmonary Doctors were arguing if that was valid or not. However, he was on full dose erythromycin that would cover that diagnosis. We could only hope for the best now. If he had a malignancy, how would anyone treat it with all this going on? Well, it was back to the board review. Maybe I would learn something that would help Billy Price. Certainly, nothing in my training so far had given me the experience to deal with such a complex situation.

Chapter 11 - Is it time to stop?

September 24th: During the week that Dr. Linke was gone, I was dealing with Dr. Patel, who inquired about whether we had a living will and indicated that we needed to begin considering if it might be time to remove Billy from the ventilator. The multiple tests being performed were not showing any infections. If this entire trauma was due to the cancer ravaging his body, Dr. Patel asked, "For what were we saving Billy?" Oh, my goodness, what an unbelievable decision to have to make. I could not comprehend making the decision to take Billy off of life support. As I agonized about this possibility throughout the day, I became more and more distraught. At one point, Lu looked me in the eyes and said to me that God was in control here. If it was not Billy's time to die there was nothing that we would do or not do that would hasten Billy's death. If we removed Billy from the respirator and it was not Billy's time, he would not die. Wow, how comforting to let go of this burden and to trust that God would be in control. Later this day just as I experienced this comfort, Dr. Patel returned to tell us that Dr. Linke had called in and told him that it was not time yet to make this decision. Until they could completely rule out involvement of infectious disease, they were to treat him aggressively.

On this day, there was a Christmas parade on the street outside the hospital presenting the MDA children's Christmas cards that they had designed. There were cars with courageous children, smiling, with IV poles and eyes seemingly bigger due to their bald heads, bands were playing, banners waving, bag pipes playing, majorettes twirling, etc…It was beautiful and amazing. Christmas in September was bigger and better than any I had witnessed before during the Christmas season. These were truly children and families living with cancer. Some would not make it until Christmas so it was time to celebrate, **now**. Wow. What a different environment in which I found myself from just a couple of weeks ago. How vividly obvious the fragility of life was. How unimportant the mundane day to day worries of the past seemed at this moment. I reflected on how the present moment was the only moment promised and how alive I felt because of this intimate knowledge.

September 25th: The next day Dr. Raed of Infectious Disease communicated that they had determined from tests that Billy had Legionnaire's Disease, a serious form of pneumonia. While this disease is serious even for a healthy individual and most likely would be fatal for someone whose health was so compromised as in Billy's situation, it actually was a relief to know that a condition that could be treatable was part of the cause of Billy's critical condition. With the benefit of this information, later that day, Dr. Patel indicated that it was not time to give up yet. They needed to give it 48 to 72 hours for the antibiotics to start to work. If things did not improve at that point, then we would discuss options.

Chapter 12 - God Provides

September 22 – October 17: Lu needed to return to North Carolina because her mother was in the final stages of pancreatic cancer and her husband, Bill, Billy's father, was recovering from a recent second heart attack. I would be alone two thousand miles from home with Billy unconscious in the ICU at the point of death when my sister, Lydia, calls to let me know she is on her way. Lydia's husband, a Methodist minister, was transferred to a new church in High Point NC just 3 months prior. At that time, Methodist ministers' tenure at their churches averaged 5 to 7 years. She had secured a new nursing position in High Point in which she was unhappy so she had quit in September and was in between jobs. This "coincidence" enabled Lydia to come to Houston to stay with me for almost a whole month at the beginning of this ordeal during a time that I was paralyzed with fear. I was not eating or sleeping well as nothing seemed to matter in the face of death. Lydia was able to help me identify and focus on what could be controlled and to learn how to participate in Billy's care which I was to learn is very important in increasing the chances for a positive outcome when dealing with serious health conditions/crises. Lydia was teaching me how to review and understand the daily lab reports, learn the questions to ask, how to talk with the doctors, walk for exercise, eat so that I could stay healthy, find cheaper housing, identify platelet donors to help with Billy's blood condition that developed, and supporting me with her love and lifting me up with her humor.

Throughout these days there was no sign that the antibiotics were working as the lab reports offered no evidence of improvement. Reversely, his condition continued to deteriorate. Billy was completely unconscious. With no communication or recognition, it no longer looked like him lying there. The doctors began to question whether Billy had Legionnaire's Disease. They said that if there was no improvement by Monday, September 29th, they would need to re-evaluate their course of treatment.

September 29th: Slight improvements were observed. We were told that contrary to their original information that the antibiotics should show results in a couple of days, they had discovered that sometimes in extreme cases it could take 2 to 3 weeks of antibiotic therapy. There was no use in attempting to stage or determine treatment for his cancer at this point because they had to treat the infection and get him stabilized first.

Chapter 13 - Angels, Angels, Everywhere

Meanwhile, Lydia and I walked every day in the park outside of the hospital and found new lodging at the EZ-8 Motel which was a 10-minute drive from the hospital. We grew to know the managers – Marguerite, Jack, and Skeet Davis. Skeet was their beagle. We moved there on September 25th and stayed until October 30th, 1991, although most of our time was at the hospital. Trips to the motel were periodic and mainly to freshen up and steal a couple of hours of sleep on a real bed.   The Davis's would transport patient's family members to MDA. During these trips, Jack would tell us stories about Skeet the Beagle which ranged from him inspecting the rooms to teaching classes at Rice University. These 10 minutes filled with humor provided an escape from the sadness and sickness. Who would think that a stranger whose purpose was to transport family members of patients could use this time to provide humor and relief? They did.

Billy's baseball team - the Atlanta Braves were in the World Series against the Minnesota Twins and Billy was missing it. Lydia and I made it back a couple of nights to see the games. What a great escape if only for a little while. Lydia and I were on the edge of the bed at the EZ-8 cheering like never before.

During the next month, we were to meet so many special people while in the ICU waiting room and the blood bank giving platelets to Billy. These included patients' families, social workers, volunteers, blood bank technicians, nurses, cab drivers, ministers, and nuns – all of whom had been strangers – that ministered to us. It is amazing how the walls that we build around ourselves come down and how much more receptive we are to others when we are in extreme circumstances. Perhaps it is because of the vulnerability of illness or in the face of death, fear of opening up to others seems so irrelevant. In any case, we found ourselves surrounded by angels who performed simple acts of love and kindness that helped to carry us through.

My friend, Kathy Brammer, called every day to check on us.

My sister, Lou, was taking care of our dogs, daily.

Blood Bank: The first time that Lydia and I gave platelets at the blood bank, Lydia had Geraldo as her technician. He was Hispanic. Lydia began to make small talk with him by asking him how long he had worked at the blood bank. Geraldo answered in broken English, "Oh this is my first time. If I do a good job, please recommend me for a position. You don't mind if I don't look. I hate to see people get stuck." Later he said, "If you have a problem, we have the solution. If you get tingly, we have Tums. If you feel faint, we have ice packs. If you are cold, we have blankets. If you die, we pull blankets over your head."

ICU Waiting Room: We met the Phillips's who were friends with Trae whose wife was in ICU too. They were going to give platelets for his wife but after her death, gave them for Billy. They chauffeured us around Houston to give us breaks from the hospital periodically.

Phyllis Neu was a regular platelet donor that we met at the Blood bank. She called almost every day and gave platelets for Billy as frequently as was medically possible. She also arranged a platelet drive for Billy.

Liza, a MDA volunteer, gave platelets, visited regularly, and also drove us around Houston.

Monica…oh Monica…she was Chilean. She was a one of the most open people I had ever met. She was blond and blue-eyed, daughter of a physician, and was raised in a German/Swiss community. One day in front of the whole ICU waiting room, she confided about her divorce, remarriage, financial ruin – they had to sell their plane – and experience with breast cancer.

My friend Tonda Shelton would quit her job and travel to Houston to be with me for several weeks off and on. She had been a friend for 16 years at this point but I discovered that you get to know people a lot better as you spend days with each other waiting around the clock. Of interest, I realized that she eats almost every hour. She was 5'11" and weighed less than 125 pounds. After watching an episode of "Bewitched", Lydia and I decided that Tonda had Veracious Ravenousitis. The ailment was Lydia's professional diagnosis which she said was common to lurches that have a protocol of "PO intake Q hourly". Obviously, we had way too much time on our hands.

Tonda became interested in the Respiratory Therapist, Gary. She asked Monica if Gary was married. This match becomes Monica's mission. Monica asked Steve, a fellow Respiratory Therapist, if Gary is married or if he is gay. Steve goes to Gary and tells him that Monica thinks he is gay. Gary then goes up to Monica and tells her that he thinks that she is gay. Thus begins the Gary/Tonda saga.

Everyone else found Tonda irresistible, such as Jeff, the physical therapist and former butcher, Joe, the blood technician, Saad, the Pathologist. Shelly, an ICU patient's family member, called her the "Erica Cane" of MD Anderson.

On one of her extended stays, both of Billy's parents were also visiting. During this time, Tonda decided to express to the Prices how much she enjoyed getting to know them before they left to go back home. She says to Lu, "I am so glad that I had the opportunity to get to know you both and I want you to know that I think you are really super." Lu looks at Bill with this puzzled look and asked, "What did she say?" Realizing that she looked puzzled, Tonda asked, "What did you think that I said?" Lu thought Tonda said that she thought they were really stupid. Aghast, Tonda said, "You thought I called you stupid?" The rest of the ICU Waiting Room heard the exchange and laughed hysterically.

Around this same time, Monica brought in Ms. Lee to the ICU waiting room, whose husband was recovering in SICU. Ms. Lee was in tears. Monica tells her that everyone in here is going through the same thing she is. At the same time, Shelly is telling the people in the waiting room about her relatives who were married in the Air Force and had to live apart for a year. Days before this exchange, Tonda had overheard Monica tell a social worker on the phone that a patient's family had some financial problems, and whispered audibly, Shelly's family name. Putting these conversations together, Tonda jumped to conclusions and shrieked, "They had to live in their car for a Year?" At this Lydia, Shelly, Tonda, and I laughed uncontrollably. Needless to say, Ms. Lee was not convinced that we shared her pain.

Chapter 14 - The Routine of Life & Death

September 21 – October 5th: It was now two weeks that Billy had been unconscious. They had to keep him asleep so that he would not be overwhelmed with pain from the pressure of the ventilator. The ventilator pressure had to be high in order to push the air into his lungs because they were so diseased. His appearance changed. He did not look like himself. It did not seem like it was him lying there.

My employer, 1st Home Federal, organized a conference call to me. They had all the employees standing around the conference room in NC when they called and prayed with me for Billy. At this moment, their love and God's presence permeated my soul.

We were continuing to stay in the ICU waiting room except during visiting hours, daily walks, or trips to the hospital cafeteria. Lydia had helped me to concentrate on what we could control. It occurred to me how adaptive the human spirit is. Within two weeks we had developed a routine and had begun to adapt to a life in crisis. Just a few weeks ago, we existed in a stable, almost normal, world. Now normal was life and death.

After about a week of limiting our time with Billy to the visiting time every 4 hours, the hospital staff began to let us come and go as we pleased. They actually began to prefer for me to be in the room because they found that Billy was less agitated and rested more peacefully. They must have realized that we had adjusted to this reality too. We were not as emotional as in the beginning faced with these circumstances and therefore would not disrupt or interfere. I would push two wooden cafeteria chairs together, curl up, and watch all of the machines that monitored his breaths, blood pressure, and heart rate. I could actually sleep even with the constant beeping and visits from the hospital staff throughout the nights. When we weren't in the room with Billy we were in the ICU waiting room with family members of the other patients. Due to the intensity of emotions and common bond that we shared, friendships were forged much more quickly than normal. Nightly around 10:00, the hospital staff would distribute blankets and pillows. The room was crowded full of couches and recliners. On any given day, there were usually around 15 of us. Jim's wife, Brenda, had been in ICU almost a week. She had leukemia. Trae's wife had been diagnosed with melanoma during pregnancy and was unable to have treatments. They determined the immediate crisis was due to toxic shock syndrome. They were in their mid-twenties and only married a couple of years. Ms. Green was probably in her 70's. Her husband, who had been treated for cancer for months, had contracted pneumonia. By this point we had shared the ICU waiting room several nights and begun to establish the pecking order of our crew. We had designated Jim as "the Head Monkey" although Mrs. Green trumped everybody. Trae was full of nervous energy and had not earned a position of authority. On the night of October 1, right before the lights were to go out, Trae started juggling shoes and doing magic tricks. Lydia and I were sleeping side by side on a foam mattress. Lydia was trying to make Trae go to sleep. Mrs. Green ordered Jim to put the towels up to cover the window on the door, which had become his job. Jim couldn't find the tape and Mrs. Green rebuked him like he was her child. When Jim taped it up it was short and light was shining through from the hallway beneath the towel. We all laughed. Mrs. Green said, "Isn't it wonderful that we can all laugh together and no one misunderstands or condemns us knowing that our loved ones are so seriously ill. "One hour later, we received a call from ICU for Mrs. Green. Her husband had died.

October 2: Jim read on his wife's lab values that most of her bone marrow was comprised of immature white blood cells known as blast cells that were crowding out the manufacture of other needed blood cells. In spite of his sorrow and sadness that night as he turned out the light, he said, "God is Good".

October 3rd: Brenda died.

October 3rd and 4th: After a few days of relative stability – if one can dare use this description for someone hanging by a thread - Billy's oxygenation saturation plummeted. His respirations increased and the pressure on the ventilator had to be increased even further. With x-rays, they were able to determine that his lungs had collapsed and so they inserted four chest tubes and put him back on 100% oxygen at high pressure levels.

Chapter 15 - Well, he is too sick to be here

September 30, 1991 thru October 6, 1991:

After the week at Harvard Oncology Review, I returned back to work on Monday. The first thing I did was go to ICU to find Billy Price. He was in room 202. It was far worse than I had imagined. He continued with fevers as high as 104 degrees every day while I was gone. He was on a ventilator and was placed on full sedation with muscle relaxants. His breathing had been so fast and labored that the respiratory machine could not keep up with him. This maneuver to sedate him did help to slow his breathing down and allow the machine to give full breaths. The ventilator was delivering oxygen at a level of 100%. He had suffered from what is called barotrauma and needed the placement of a chest tube. Barotrauma is when pressure in the lungs from the ventilator is too high and the lungs form a hole and the lung collapses. The chest tube is to reverse pressure within the chest cavity to allow the lungs to expand back to normal. His chest X-ray was showing more changes with more infiltrates suggesting the infection was actually worse. I talked with the Pulmonary Physician and he was cautious with his recovery, although they felt they were doing the right thing for his treatment. They were convinced that the Legionnaire's disease diagnosis was correct. Infectious Disease service related that it may take 3 to 4 weeks to show recovery from the infection. Billy was receiving multiple antibiotics now including Primaxin, Bactrim, Erythromycin and Rifampin. Both services were cautious with any optimism as his lungs were severely ill by Chest X-ray with all the areas showing congestion of the lungs and possible scarring. Maybe Billy contracted the infection while at the hospital in North Carolina. It is hard to tell with the possibility of infection being earlier than his admission to the hospital. At that point, there was one chest tube placed. Over the course of the next month, he would require four more chest tubes to be placed to expand his lungs back open from areas of collapsing by new events of barotrauma. A total of five chest tubes were placed while Billy was on the ventilator. Would Billy be able to survive several more weeks at this rate with a cancer process in the picture?

I went in to examine him and there were some changes on the exam from the first day I met him. The lymph nodes were now gone in the left collar bone area and the mass under the left arm was smaller. His condition was so precarious that it would be impossible to move him to the Radiology department for a CT-Scan test to confirm that. Even the nurses in the Intensive Care Unit wondered if he could be moved from the unit. **"Why would he be moved", I asked. Well, he is too sick to be here. The patient being too sick I could relate to, but where else could I put him?**

With these lymph node and masses smaller, how would I get a good biopsy? What had caused their reduction in size? Is that an effect of the prednisone or a treatment effect of the antibiotics? I would have to think about that further, although my suspicion was it was due to the prednisone. In discussion with the Infectious Disease physicians they felt the lymph nodes could be enlarged by the infection but not to the extent we had seen in the presenting CT-Scan. Regardless, his ability to take treatment for any cancer would be limited with the pneumonia and lung condition. His lung status was worsening and he was now in Adult Respiratory Distress Syndrome, which basically happens when the lungs are unable to get enough oxygen into the body and unable to remove the carbon dioxide. It can progress into scarring of the lung tissue causing complete lung failure. There was a major possibility that even the ventilator would not be enough to sustain his life.

Additionally, over that prior week, his platelet count dropped drastically from a normal number of 250,000 upon admission to as low as 6,000. Platelets are the blood cells that help stop bleeding events and form clots or scabs. Could the lowered platelet count be related to medications, to the underlying malignancy, to a bone marrow process with the malignancy or another cause such as the overwhelming stress of the lung condition? Dr. Patel had a bone marrow biopsy performed on Friday, September 27th. Billy had been receiving platelet transfusions with some benefit but clearly no platelet count recovery was being seen at this time. He also became quite anemic and required several blood transfusions as well. I wondered if he had been bleeding. Most likely these problems were either a medication issue or related to overwhelming stress on the bone marrow to make normal blood cells. I reviewed the list of medications and thinned it out as much as possible. If these problems related to the cancer process, there was nothing to do at this point, with his overall condition and no real diagnosis of the cancer process.

I called Pathology to see if they had any better idea what the malignancy was on the biopsy material done in North Carolina. The best they could call the malignancy from the left arm area was going to be called an unclassified malignancy of undetermined origin, suspecting a high-grade sarcoma. Well that didn't help very much, although I understood their inability to be more specific.

If the lowered platelet count was due to the overwhelming condition and stresses, we were doing what we could to treat those. The possibility of bleeding is a major concern with low platelets. He could bleed from the lungs and the chest tube sites, from an ulcer in the stomach, or basically anywhere. With the prednisone on board, I would be most concerned about an ulcer bleeding. He did have a nasogastric tube which is a tube running through his nose to drain the stomach contents and certainly that could cause trauma to the lining of the stomach as well. With all this stress, who wouldn't have an ulcer? He was on medication though to reduce the risk of that possibility. From looking at the contents that drained from his stomach he did have a small amount of blood from stomach, but nothing major at this time.

The bone marrow biopsy and aspiration were performed to see if that would diagnose the cause of the lowered platelets. Several days later, the bone marrow report showed normal platelet production and no evidence of malignancy. That was good news overall, but still didn't explain the problem with the lowered platelet counts and the lowered red blood counts and anemia. It didn't add any help in his diagnosis either. What was the malignancy? Luckily, although only a small relief, it didn't involve the bone marrow at this time.

The good news was over the next week his fever did start to reduce. From temperatures that were reaching 104 twice a day, he was now running below 100 degrees most of the time. That allowed me to lower his prednisone dosing and make a determination if the fevers had related to the Legionnaire's infection or could be related to the cancer process itself. Some malignancies can have fevers as part of their presentation, such as Hodgkin's Disease, Non-Hodgkin's Lymphoma and certain types of Leukemia. The Infectious Disease Service did start to adjust and remove some of the antibiotic coverage believing that the Erythromycin was the drug that would offer the most help at this time.

Chapter 16 - Living in Crisis:

Creating a routine and focusing on what could be controlled was helpful. Cards were coming in by the handfuls daily. The daily visit to the hospital post office was a highlight. Most of the cards were from strangers from my brother-in-law, Ken Lyon's, church in High Point which I had never attended. I began to post them on the walls of the ICU room, which I am sure was a fire hazard but no one had the heart to tell me. By the time we were to leave, there were over 500 cards papering the wall. They enveloped us in love.

Various people gave me suggestions on what to do when caring for someone that was comatose. These included:

- Playing soothing music to create a calming environment to drown out the drone of the ICU bells and alarms. I knew that Billy would have preferred Rick James' "Super Freak" but he wasn't getting his way this time.
- Talking to the patient as if they are awake about all of the things important to them

such as conversations with family and friends, current events, and sports
- Reading the USA Today Sports section and talking to him about our football pool. My brother, Clyde, made this suggestion.
- Learning the lab values and tracking the blood counts, daily, such as the bilirubin (liver), white blood cells (infection), platelets (clotting factor), red blood cells (oxygen level), creatinine and blood urea nitrogen (kidneys), and blood gases (oxygenation).

I also read a book entitled, "Head First" by Norman Cousins which described the spiritual and physical ways to encourage healing for those with serious illnesses and how important it is to have a good relationship with the physicians and for the active participation of the patient and family in the process. We learned how important it is to understand the disease and to ask questions.

Lydia and I went to the hospital library to read up on his final diagnosis which was Aggressive Large Cell Diffuse Histiocytic Lymphoma.

Dr. Linke would often visit while I was reading the sports section of the USA today, which I would read to Billy from cover to cover every day. I was to learn that she was a real sports fanatic especially for the Dallas Cowboys and Ohio State, her alma mater. She began to linger in the room with me to look at the upcoming NFL football games. We would digress on the quarterbacks, the mood of the team, and injuries and try to predict the outcomes. I had always been intimidated by doctors, but Dr. Linke was becoming my friend. It was hard to believe that we were the same age.

Chapter 17 - Spiritual Digression:

Knowing that Billy's life was in the balance, I felt the responsibility to prepare his soul for death if that was to be his imminent fate. While I still believed God's message that he had given me, I also knew there was no physical evidence, and I felt that we needed to be prepared for the worst. I knew that he was a Christian but we had not discussed his relationship with God and his thoughts on death and eternal life. Being 2000 miles from home we did not have a local minister. Raised in a Methodist Minister's home, I had been blessed with a strong spiritual foundation but I was not trained in how to help someone die and prepare their soul for eternity. I felt inadequate but there was no time for insecurity. I decided that since Billy couldn't speak with God directly, I would somehow need to intercede. I began placing my hand on Billy and asking God to save his soul...to reconcile any unresolved issues. I asked God to bless the room, the walls, the equipment, the doctors and nurses, and all of those who entered the room. I asked that it would be a sacred place and that everyone who entered would feel God's presence. I prayed this prayer continuously so much that the room felt sacred. I asked God to heal Billy's broken body and to use the medicines to eat away at the cancer. I envisioned it being eaten away like the video game, Pac Man.

I would place my hand on Billy and recite the following verses:
- "He will keep thee at perfect peace whose mind is stayed on thee?" (Isaiah 26:3)
- "My peace I leave with you. My peace I give to you. Not as the world gives, give I only unto you. Neither let your heart be troubled neither let it be afraid (John 14:27). "...and, lo I am with you always even 'til the end of time." (Matthew 28:20)

These scriptures calmed both of us.

I began reading books that people recommended. One was one on Christian Science. The precepts with which I did not totally agree, but the spiritual concepts, I did. As with everything else during this time, every word was alive and meaningful. There was clarity in my spirituality, faith, and God, and it permeated every moment.

Chapter 18 - "Now Hope is for what we cannot see."

As the intensity of the circumstances increased, the occurrences of the random acts of kindness and special moments described earlier happened more frequently, probably because of the higher level of consciousness that accompanies emergencies and because God knew that we needed these moments due to the increased desperation created by the conditions.

Emotions were high during this time. Lydia had been my stronghold but the stress was wearing her down. I had been inside these hospital walls for several days. I kept reflecting back on the message that God gave me on the plane trip to Houston that Billy would be healed. So much had happened. When each moment is life and death, it makes the time go much slower. It seemed like we had been there forever. I felt such comfort when I received that message on the plane trip out to MD Anderson and kept getting assurances that God was working in the midst of these dire circumstances but I began to question if I got the message wrong. Things had gone from bad to worse. A glimmer of hope would be followed by a new, different, and more serious crisis. Even a social worker had expressed concern about my mental state because I seemed to be in denial about the gravity of Billy's condition. It was during this time that I ventured outside for a breath of fresh air and found myself beside the calming sounds of the fountain just outside the hospital. I was at the end of my rope...exhausted due to the constant run of adrenaline that the situation caused. I asked God if I had misunderstood His message. Had He meant that Billy would be healed in heaven? I was so tired and I simply asked God to give me strength. Immediately, I could feel God fill me with His power and felt an assurance that I could face anything with HIM.

During this time Lydia kept saying, I am afraid that all these measures are being taken to save his life, but for what are we saving him? What if all of the symptoms are due to the cancer? If it is all due to the cancer and there is no chance for a remission or any quality of life, why are we putting him through this? I remember Lydia kept asking this over and over to the point that it started to annoy me.

I had certain scriptures that I had been focusing on that brought me comfort. One of them was Romans 8:28, "And we know that all things work together for good to them that love God, to them who are the called according to his purpose."

But on this day, I dropped back to verses 24 and 25…Now Hope that is seen is not Hope. For who hopes for what he sees? For if we hope for what we cannot see, we wait for it with patience. (Romans 8: 24-25) Suddenly it occurred to me that I was living hope. I knew hope in a close and personal way that I would never have known otherwise. Lydia wanted evidence for hope and she wanted it now but hope is for what you cannot see and the evidence comes in its own time.

October 5th: On this morning I entered into Billy's room expecting to see him unresponsive as he had been for 2 weeks when he looks up at me with the ventilator tube in his mouth, he smiled and winked at me. He formed a kiss as best he could around the tube of the ventilator. Oh my goodness, words once again cannot describe the elation seeing the recognition in his eyes and to know that he was still in there. It was still my Billy letting me know he was ok, if only for that moment. I ran out of the room to the ICU waiting room to let everyone know that Billy had kissed at me.

October 8th: By Monday morning, his oxygen saturation and breathing had improved some with the tubes. Finally, the Legionnaire's appeared to be dissipating - the first positive signs. They had not even attempted to assess the cancer at this point because Billy had been so critical that all of their time had been focused on trying to get him over the infection. They were trying to wean him from the ventilator so that they could treat the cancer now. With this improvement, they decided to perform another bronchoscope to assess the condition of his lungs.

October 13th: My best friend, Tonda Shelton, had been calling me almost every day. She was working at a job that was really stressful. She was having a hard time accepting how upset her boss would become over everything especially when comparing the situation to one of a life and death struggle as was Billy's. When faced with another fit from her boss this day, she gave him some instruction on what he could do with the job, faxed him her resignation, and hopped a plane to Houston. Wow…what a friend. She "happened" to arrive 4 days before Lydia had to go back. God says that he will not give us more than we can handle. Being 2000 miles from home for an uncertain period of time in such a precarious situation could have been unbearable, but amazingly, I was never alone, spiritually or physically. It is unbelievable that people were able to leave their home and be with me for extended periods of time but their love coupled with life's circumstances enabled them to come at exactly the time that they were needed during this ordeal.

Chapter 19 - Can It Get Any Worse?

October 7, 1991 thru October 14, 1991: The week started with the elation that Billy Price had survived another week. Although he remained on full ventilator support and was completely sedated, his chest x-ray was actually starting to show some improvement. Elation over that news changed drastically by midday. His platelet counts remained low requiring daily platelet transfusions.

I received a call from the Pulmonary Doctor that had done the first bronchoscope. He related a concern to me that Billy's airway pressures had drastically risen over the last 2 days. I was trying to comprehend this information when he related to me that it most likely reflected progressive scarring in the lungs caused by the lung trying to heal the infection and being on the ventilator and aggressive oxygen support. Despite all the treatment he remained on 60% oxygen levels by the ventilator. He related that his process was unlikely to be reversible. I did relate that I had lowered his prednisone last week and he felt that an increase in the dose of that drug might help. I asked if any other testing could be done to find the cause. He related that a bronchoscope might help to look at the major airways again and a possible lung biopsy might be in order. I asked him he would proceed with the bronchoscope and he related it was scheduled for the next day. I appreciated him for his diligence and willingness to proceed in such a difficult case.

I went to Billy's room to find his wife, Leah. She was there and understandably quite distraught over the information she was told about the lung airway pressures. She was aware that it meant that the machine had to work much harder to get the air into the lungs. The lungs were becoming less compliant and didn't expand as well. I tried to assure her that we were doing the testing that might offer better care. Maybe I was trying to assure myself, as well.

If the lungs were so damaged, his ability to get back off the ventilator at any time would be quite low. We didn't discuss the possibility of removing the ventilator. It is a process no one wants to be involved in at any time. I had been through that situation before with my own family members and with other patients, and it is very emotional for all the parties involved. The best I could offer at that time was that the bronchoscope would hopefully clarify the situation. I was less sure it would offer any hope at all for a reversal of the process his lungs were going through.

The next day, I received a call from the Pulmonologist. He seemed quite excited to inform me about the bronchoscope procedure findings. That seemed odd at the time, since I had prepared myself for terrible news. He related to me that a new mass was found in the airway blocking the left main stem bronchus. I closed my eyes and tried to picture what he was telling me. A mass? A mass within the airway? A mass within the airway blocking the left lung passageway? I tried to imagine what was causing this and how did it grow up so fast? I calmly asked, "Were you able to biopsy it?"

The Pulmonologist replied that he felt uncomfortable proceeding with a biopsy due to his lowered platelet count that was around 39,000 that morning. I was pleased that he felt that a biopsy would be helpful and asked him if I could get some platelet transfusions available, would he plan to proceed with a biopsy. While platelet transfusions are quite common to be used today, using them in 1991 was far more complicated and needed more time to get them ready. I talked to our Blood Bank and they informed me they could have the platelet product ready for the procedure within the week. After a quick call back to the Pulmonologist, I felt better that we were looking into this new development so rapidly.   Could this be the break in this case that we needed or could this be the problem that we couldn't solve?

The week continued on with more issues of the airway pressures rising. His ventilator had been adjusted to increase the pressure of the air being forced from the machine into the lung. This can cause more of the lung traumas we had already dealt with. Not surprisingly, more chest tubes were placed at this time to keep the lungs expanded and reverse the collapsing of the lungs. I was able to review the pictures that were placed in the chart of the airway during the second bronchoscope and indeed within the last three weeks a round, red fleshy lump had developed in the airway. It was easy to see that it blocked the whole round passageway to the left lung. I looked back at the picture of that area taken just 3 weeks earlier. Nothing was there at that time. Now, a mass took up that whole space. Certainly, this was not Legionnaire's disease. Hopefully, the biopsy would tell us what had been going on all along, since the original lump under the left arm was found. Even for me, finding a lump in the airway confused the whole picture again. For a sarcoma to involve the lungs, it is usually round masses in the lung itself, but not in the airways. This mass in the airway would most resemble a true bronchial carcinoma or lung cancer. But that diagnosis is not likely in a 34-year-old man who is not a smoker. And if this was lung cancer, why wasn't it there on the first bronchoscope? However, I went back to my original thought this could be a lymphoma, but that didn't make a lot of sense to me either. During the time he was on prednisone, his lymph nodes actually diminished in size. Prednisone is a common drug used it the treatment of many lymphomas for its direct effect to reduce lymphoma cells. Was a whole new process going on? That seemed impossible to understand or imagine that any one patient could be so unlucky.

Chapter 20 - The Diagnosis

October 15, 1991 thru October 22, 1991: This week seemed to move so slowly. It started with the bronchoscope of the lung with the planned biopsy. Luckily, the platelet transfusion was not needed as Billy's platelet count had fully recovered. While the biopsy went well, the waiting for the biopsy answer was quite distressing. I understood that it would take time to process the material correctly and that this material may be just as difficult to discern for pathology answer as the first biopsy. That didn't make the wait any easier, while Billy's lungs continued with such distress.

Fortunately, we had an excellent Pathology Department at M.D. Anderson and I felt sure they would finally clarify the situation. In the meantime, Billy was not faring well with his lung situation. While the fevers had diminished, his lungs continued to need higher air pressure to deliver the amount of oxygen his body needed. It was concerning that when we needed an answer the quickest; it seemed to take the longest. Daily, I would call the pathology department and would hear the same answer that they were working on the material and needed further testing to finalize a diagnosis. This step can take days to a week and less commonly even longer, depending on the staining and processing of the material that is needed. With the advances seen today, most biopsy materials are sent through several panels of testing to be assured of the correct diagnosis.

Another event occurred during this wait. Billy started to have increased fevers again. After cultures of blood and urine, it was found he was growing a fungal infection. He was started on Amphotericin. It can cause issues of fevers itself and a shaking syndrome while being infused. It wasn't called Shake 'N Bake for nothing by medical professionals and patients alike. It was not surprising that a fungal infection could arise in such an ill patient who had been on so many antibiotics and prednisone over the last several months and with so many procedures, central intravenous lines, chest tubes, a tube to the stomach, and a tube to the lungs.

One afternoon after finishing clinic, I went down to Billy's room to see him. It was a rare event to find Billy alone in his room. Usually a nurse and at least one family member or friend was there. I couldn't blame them for being away from this. I couldn't imagine sitting so diligent at his bedside day and night. I noticed that a radio was on and playing Poke Salad Annie. I then realized that Billy was tapping his left foot to the beat of the music. While I wanted to make sure he was sedated appropriately, I smiled at his ability to enjoy the beat of the music. I talked to the nurse and we increased the medication to allow him to be asleep.

It was now a week from the biopsy of the airway mass. Even I was getting frustrated. Daily, the family would want to know of any results. Knowing the original material was difficult to make a diagnosis, maybe the next material would result in the same confusing answer. Finally, on October 22, the pathologist called and felt sure that the biopsy showed a Diffuse Ki-1 positive, Large B Cell Non-Hodgkin's Lymphoma. While it certainly fit well with most of the clinical events we had seen.   Now the process of deciding on treatment, if any, would begin. For over 6 weeks, I had avoided the issue of treatment of the cancer, due to the overwhelming lung issues with Legionnaire's disease and Adult Respiratory Distress Syndrome.

Chapter 21 - Prayer for Intervention – I didn't mean for anyone to get hurt

October 15th: The bronchoscope was done to perform a biopsy. Dr. Linke indicated that they needed new tissue to confirm the type and stage of cancer.

October 22nd: The pulmonologist told us that the biopsy indicated that the blockage in the airways was lymphoma, not sarcoma. Again, they wanted to continue to wean him from the ventilator before giving him chemo. Dr. Linke came by later this day to let me know that with the change in diagnosis they were going to need to transfer Billy's care to a lymphoma specialist. I begged her to keep Billy in her care. I had such confidence in her willingness to treat Billy aggressively despite how futile it seemed. I did not want anyone else. She told me that it was in Billy's best interest to have someone specialized in treatment of his kind of cancer. That night I desperately prayed to God to somehow intervene and keep Dr. Linke on the case.

October 23rd: Dr. Linke comes by this day to let me know that there has been a change in plans. She will be staying on the case. The new specialist assigned to Billy's case had to suddenly leave for Venezuela. His father had contracted high altitude sickness while climbing a mountain there. Oh my goodness, I felt really bad. God had answered my prayers but I did not mean for anyone to get hurt.

Chapter 22 - "Later" had arrived

As Billy Price's doctor, the decision to treat Billy would not be an easy one. On one hand, Billy had a very treatable and possibly curable malignancy. On its own, a Diffuse Large B-Cell Lymphoma had a good chance at full remission at that time with a combination of drugs called CHOP-B given every 3 weeks. For the patient with this disease and far better health condition, this treatment is given as an outpatient and overall tolerated well. The patient can easily be home that night after chemotherapy is given and do follow ups to the office for blood count checks. Billy was not that patient.

CHOP-B was a combination of drugs that included Cyclophosphamide, Adriamycin, Oncovin, Prednisone and Bleomycin. Usually the acronyms of the drug combinations reflect very well the drugs used. It is a long explanation to why the H is used for Adriamycin. Briefly, it reflects the chemical name. Based on well-respected clinical trials and long term follow up on Diffuse Large B-cell Lymphomas at that time, his complete remission rate with this treatment was 75%. A long-term chance of staying in remission was 25% at 5 years.

Today the front-line treatment of choice would be CHOP-R, which uses the previously mentioned CHOP with a newer agent called Rituxan, instead of Bleomycin. Rituxan is an immune modifier that targets lymphoma cells that carry a marker called CD 20. It has increased the remission and survival rates in many types of lymphomas without adding a lot to the toxicities of the treatment.

On the other hand, CHOP is given in lymphoma therapy every 3 weeks with the expected complications of lowered blood counts, such as lowered white blood counts, that help fight infection and lowered red cell counts making patients mare anemic and fatigued. The combination can also lower platelet counts and as already discussed, that was an issue that had started before any chemotherapy was initiated although appeared resolved at this time. The issue of infection remained a major concern with the issues of the lung infection and the need for a central line to be in place to feed Billy with Nutritional Support and to give antibiotics. The central lines we used in those days were introduced through the skin and protruded out with a catheter that allowed the medications to be given. The problem with these lines is they need to be checked for infection and removed and replaced on a regular basis to lower the infection risk. We had already been through several catheter replacements and infections of those catheters. How many more complications could this patient handle? When would an infection arise that wouldn't respond to antibiotics?

At this juncture, I had a treatable cancer in a patient that was clearly not ready for any treatment I could offer. The dilemma was quite problematic and in discussion with both Pulmonary and Infectious Disease specialists they wanted an extra week to try to get Billy ready for any therapy. They felt the infections would be better controlled and his lungs may show some recovery. Maybe they were hoping a week would prove any chemotherapy was not possible at all. Neither physician seemed too encouraged that a week would make a difference. None the less, I was obligated to tell Leah and Billy's family the biopsy results and give recommendations.

I found Leah with her friends in the ICU waiting room. They were working on pumpkins that they were decorating for the Halloween Pumpkin Contest. This didn't seem like the appropriate time to bring up chemotherapy. Well, I guess it was a good as any other time. I am not sure what I would have decided if this was my family. I always felt I would have done as much as possible for a younger patient like Billy. To this day, I have no idea at where I would cut off the age for giving therapy. As medical advances have come along, that age range is gradually increasing with an older population receiving chemotherapy with less complications and with an aging population that is in far better health overall.

I sat down and asked if we could talk about Billy's case. The ICU waiting room was basically Leah and her friends that night. They seemed to be in a happy mood with trying to come up with different ideas on decorating the pumpkins. They felt they could do better than Rapunzel. I related that a diagnosis was finally made on the biopsy of the mass in the lung airway. I reported that they were calling it a moderately aggressive form of Large B-Cell Non-Hodgkin's Lymphoma. I went on to describe that the treatment is usually chemotherapy and possibly irradiation treatments. I related that I felt we should have a Lymphoma Specialist, of which we had a department of physicians qualified to treat lymphoma to take over the case. I assured them that they didn't have to make a decision on treatment this evening, but time was of the essence as so much time had passed since the start of this whole process. I asked that they allow me to consult with the Lymphoma Service. Surprisingly, that did not go over well at all.

Leah was convinced that I needed to care for Billy's Lymphoma. I was shocked to think that in a 6-week period they had decided I needed to care for Billy. I related that my specialization was now in the sarcoma department and I felt that his case would be better handled by doctors that had years of experience with this lymphoma. At that point, I didn't have years of experience of treating any cancer. Most service times with any particular type of cancer or family of cancers lasted about two months. Leah remained adamant that I remain on the case with Billy.

I reflected and realized that in the past 6 weeks, I had asked Pulmonary and Infectious Disease specialists to care for him. They had diagnosed the infection and had basically cared for him in most of the critical situations. I had never really made any major decisions except to keep the group working on the process at hand and offer support to Leah and her friends and family that came to visit. Over those days, I had become closer to Leah Price, his wife. She had found a local hotel after camping out in Billy's room for the first several weeks. She was now close to the hospital and some of their friends would come and visit when possible. It was Billy's Mom that had come along with them originally but she had already returned to North Carolina to help care for her husband. Bill Price, Billy's Father, who suffered from heart disease and he had recently had a second heart attack. I am sure Billy's parents wanted to be in Houston as much as possible.

I found out from Leah that Billy's favorite football team was oddly enough the Houston Oilers. I still wonder how one becomes a fan of a Houston team while growing up in North Carolina. Our routine became reviewing the x-rays, labs, medications, and checking his fevers and vital signs. We would discuss what treatments were needed such as platelet transfusions or the need for bronchoscope and any new test results. After checking Billy over, we would put the sports page on Billy's lap in his hospital bed and review the National Football League line up for the upcoming weekend. Over the season, we learned the starting quarterbacks, the head coaches, and the owners of all the teams. Even though I am a Dallas Cowboy fan, it became easy to cheer the Houston Oilers. Unfortunately for Billy, he was missing one of the best seasons the Houston Oilers had in their history while based in Houston. Before I left the room, I would fold up the newspaper and tell Billy to get well.

I would end our talk with saying that I believed the treatment was the best we could offer and the hope remained that his lungs would recover enough to work on the malignancy later.

"Later" had arrived. The malignancy that had presented with no confirmed diagnosis, no completed staging to find out how extensive it was, and no real chance at treatment, now had a diagnosis and a treatment option.

Chapter 23 - Lucky Star

I am to find out several months later that the pathologist who performed the original diagnosis back in Greensboro, NC was married to one of my co-workers. When he found out that MDA determined that Billy had been misdiagnosed with sarcoma and it was in fact Lymphoma, he told his wife that there was no way that he got it wrong. The real "coincidence" though was that if Billy had not been "misdiagnosed", he would not have been referred to a teaching hospital. The only reason we were sent to another treatment center was because of the rarity of the type of cancer with which he was originally diagnosed. If Billy had stayed in Greensboro, he would have died from the Legionnaires. Because the physicians in Greensboro were convinced that all of the infectious symptoms were due to the cancer they were not conducting any further tests or prescribing any antibiotics at all.

October 29th: Severe de-saturation prompted another bronchoscope which revealed that the cancer was spreading rapidly. Dr. Peters indicated that they would not be able to wean him from the ventilator before starting chemo as they had hoped. Chemo is dangerous anyway, nevertheless, when a patient is already compromised and on a ventilator with four chest tubes. Normally the patient's white blood cells and platelets have to be at acceptable levels. When the blood counts drop there is a danger of bleeding and infection. Dr. Linke came by later this day to ask me what I wanted to do. She said with the cancer growing so rapidly it would close off his airway very soon. Without treatment death would be imminent. She said that if they give him chemo with him so sick and so many ports for entry of germs, he most likely would die of an infection. In my mind, there was no choice. At least with treatment there was a chance. She said…" maybe he will have a lucky star".

Seven days after it was started, the chemo had begun to destroy Billy's white blood cells and platelets. Because of this he would become more susceptible to infections and internal bleeding. His platelets had dropped to less than 4000 which created a serious danger of bleeding internally. We discovered that Billy's platelets rebounded much better to single donor platelets than it did to random donor platelets which were comprised of platelets from several donors. During this time, we became acquainted with Phyllis who donated platelets at the blood bank. Lydia had Phyllis to begin giving platelets for Billy. She was a lovely lady who worked at an oil company as an executive secretary for the VP of Human Resources. We met a couple of ministers who visited the hospital regularly. Bob was crippled. We met Dane Lee whose grandfather was in SICU. She was 19 and was a real firecracker. We learned that she had several operations on her stomach. She showed us the deep scars. Her parents were divorced when she was 6 or 7. Her father is wealthy, but neither has offered much security or stability. Most of the time we never know the struggles that others have endured.

Chapter 24 - Good Luck

Despite Leah's clear reluctance to let another doctor take over the care of Billy's Lymphoma, I was able to persuade her that a Lymphoma specialist would be good in his care plan in order to make sure the treatments were on target and to offer me advice when situations were complicated. Could Billy's case get more complicated? Well, in all honesty, why not?

I am sure there were many times Leah felt overwhelmed with the information coming from so many different doctors at the hospital. There were times she would get conflicting information and it became my job to sort that out for her or clarify why two physicians would have different ideas on the same situation. For myself, a physician that had just completed fellowship training, this became quite overwhelming to me. My head of the Department of Sarcoma became a good person to ask for advice. But as the weeks went on I felt more compelled that I could handle most situations on my own. In the situation of deciding on chemotherapy treatment, I was less sure.

I headed over the Lymphoma Section. Having trained at M. D. Anderson, I had an idea who might be able to offer help and an idea of who I might like involved in this case. Perhaps I was just hoping someone else would take over and I wouldn't have to carry the heavy burden anymore. I sat in the conference room and several physicians of the lymphoma group were there with other Fellows on service. They were discussing cases and were agreeable to hear about this case. I described Billy's complex case of the lung condition, being on full ventilator support, and the known extent of the lymphoma including the airway mass along with the pathologic diagnosis recently made.

They asked very few questions. They related that CHOP-Bleomycin would be the treatment of choice. I wondered if the Bleomycin should be used here since it has a known complication of lung damage. They advised that it could be left out in this case. I asked if they would be willing to see him. They basically told me they could do a consult and as I left I heard one of them say, "Good Luck."

I went back to the ICU and related to Leah that I was going to ask for a formal consult from the Lymphoma Section. I was fortunate to have Dr. William Velasquez see him in consultation. He confirmed what I knew. A Large B-Cell Lymphoma would be best treated by CHOP, leave out the Bleomycin, and be ready for complications. I had hoped he would be able to take over his case, but that seemed unlikely.

I asked Leah what she thought of having Dr. Velasquez taking over the care of Billy and his Lymphoma. She remained reluctant to change her position in this situation. I was going to have to care for Billy and his Lymphoma. She had no trouble with me asking advice from others.

I went to my Head of Department and described to him the situation at this time. He had seen Billy a few times throughout the weeks when he was on call. He clearly knew how ill Billy was but he felt Billy deserved a chance at getting better. We discussed the treatment and decided on CHOP as the first therapy to be used with another option of therapy to use, if needed. With his support, I felt strong enough to proceed with talking more formally about the care of Billy's Lymphoma.

Through this week, the Pulmonary Service had wanted to see if the ventilator support could be lessened. They were concerned about the amount of oxygen being used and the pressure needed on the lungs. I related that we were thinking of starting chemotherapy and they had a major concern on how it would be tolerated, but honestly, now I felt that Billy had nothing to lose.

I went to discuss the chemotherapy further with Leah. While I felt assured that the treatment was an excellent choice and offered a great chance of getting better, I remained very concerned that a complication could be insurmountable. It could be a bleed that might be impossible to control. Perhaps an infection comes along and is unable to be treated fully. Even more likely, the lymphoma is too advanced and the chemotherapy wouldn't be enough to make him better. I tried to paint a realistic picture although I have learned over the years, you can never paint that realism too well. It is difficult for us to imagine someone being that sick. Conversely, it was equally difficult to imagine Billy getting sicker.

I allowed Leah to ask questions. I am not sure what I really said that convinced her we should proceed because I truly painted a picture of little hope and a minuscule chance of a good outcome. For all to fall into place, he needed the treatment to work to its best and be lucky enough to have no new major complications. It was hard to imagine his situation would allow no further complications. While I knew a 34-year man in decent health could tolerate the planned chemotherapy well, it was difficult to figure out how he would tolerate the treatment with all these issues already in place.

Leah felt that she wanted to proceed with chemotherapy for Billy, but wanted to think about it for a bit. I related that we needed to proceed as soon as possible with the lung and airway situation being so precarious now. She was going to talk to Billy's family and let me know in the morning.

The next day, the Pulmonary Physician related he was planning another bronchoscope procedure because he was concerned about the airway being in more distress. He found out on that testing that the mass had enlarged significantly since the one done on October 8th. They had also decided to do a tracheotomy procedure on October 25th. This would place the tube to his lungs at the neck area rather than having to go from the nose and through the back of the throat. This would reduce the area of airflow travel by a considerable amount. Hopefully this might help the ventilator support Billy's breathing. The Pulmonologist advice at this time was to proceed with treatment as soon as possible as the airway mass had continued to grow.

The day had come to make a final decision. I talked again to Leah. It was clear she had searched her options and talked to family and friends. She was convinced she needed to try treatment for the Lymphoma. Without treatment, it was clear he would succumb to the lymphoma and the stressors on his lungs. To be honest, what did she have to lose in this situation? Pulmonary had advised her that the lung condition would not worsen with chemotherapy and without chemotherapy his survival was measured in days to weeks. With little to lose and perhaps everything to gain, we started chemotherapy. When I told the ICU Nurses that we planned chemotherapy to start in the morning, their response was, "Why are you doing that?" I related with a 75% chance of remission, Billy deserved at least a chance to improve. I am sure they were not convinced.

Chapter 25 - Treatment begins

October 25: They performed a tracheotomy to take the tube out of Billy's mouth and put it in his neck.

October 30 – November 6: Even at a world-renowned hospital like MD Anderson, they had never given chemo to someone while on a respirator, not to mention 4 chest tubes, catheter, central line, and a feeding tube – multiple sites for entry of infection. But it is under these circumstances that Billy's first treatment began this day. His white blood cells, red blood cells, and platelet counts started to fall around day 7. Normal platelet levels are 250,000. His dropped to 2000. Internal bleeding became a real danger. He continued to be fully sedated and unresponsive. Between 8 and 11 days from treatment he became agitated, started to cough incessantly, and began to bleed in his lungs.

November 1: Lydia had found out about 8 apartments located about a mile from the hospital that were rent-free that were available to cancer patients and their families who were having extended treatments at MD Anderson. She put us on a waiting list and one became open on November 1st. I packed up the few clothes that I had bought from Target and moved in. Even though I would continue to stay at the hospital most days, it was a place to escape for a real shower and a nap. These walks to the hospital were refreshing even though it was steaming hot in Houston, even in November. I did not know until later that this was a high crime area in which people dared not to walk.

November 17: Today was Billy's birthday. What do you do to commemorate a birthday for someone that is unconscious in ICU in critical condition? Do you celebrate? Lydia and I wondered what others would think if we had a party then decided what does it matter what others think. Billy was still alive and that is something to celebrate. We got him a cake. We went to the gift shop and got balloons and birthday hats and had a birthday party.

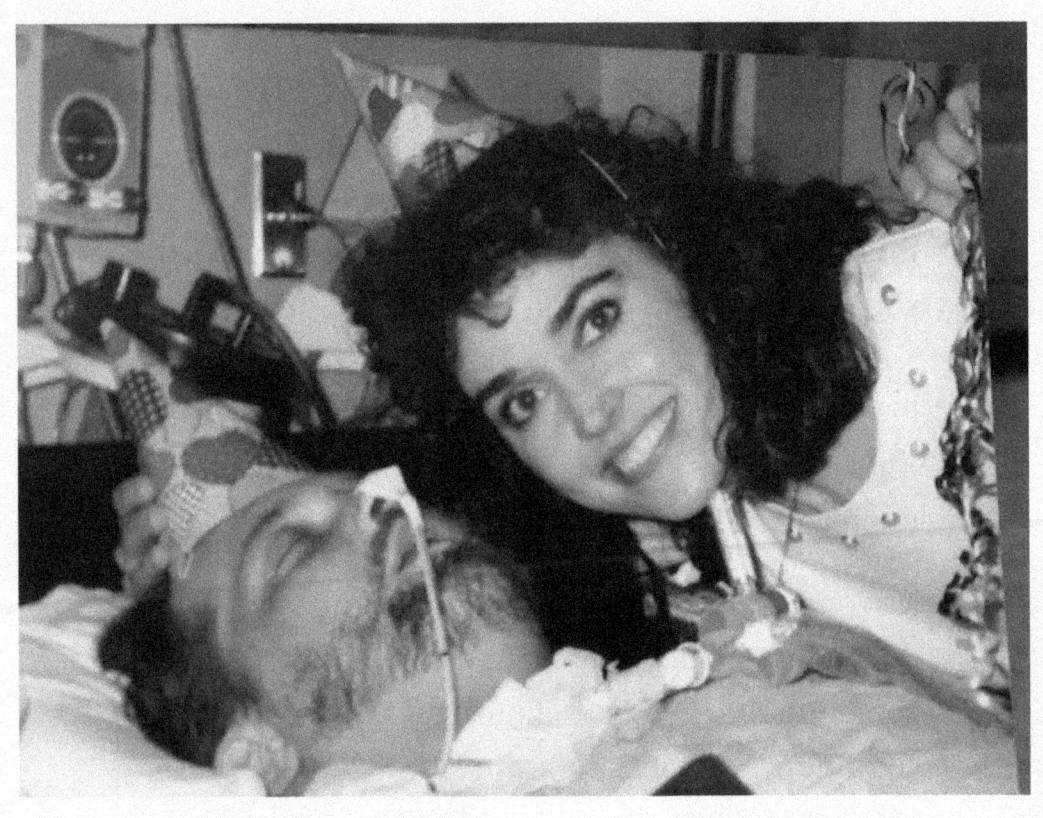

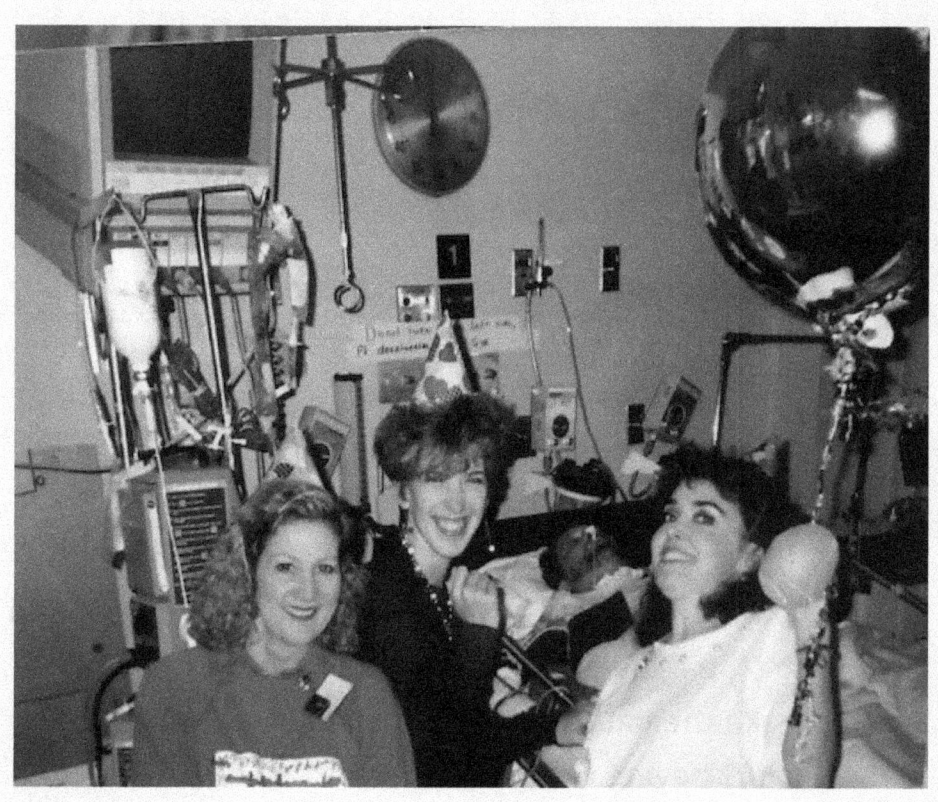

Chapter 26 - Do or Die

October 30: The first day of chemotherapy finally arrived. I ordered the medications and planned for the worse. CHOP was ordered at standard doses along with nausea medications to prevent nausea. One of the major complications of chemotherapy is nausea. I had no idea how a patient fully asleep on a ventilator would respond to the issue of nausea. Would all the sedation take the nausea out of the picture or would he start having vomiting while asleep on a ventilator? Vomiting into the airway that he couldn't protect could cause an aspiration into the lungs. That would be the last thing his lung condition needed.

I was concerned over the management of his blood counts especially in view of the issue of the lowered platelet count that previously developed. He had already received blood and platelet transfusions and may need more of those after chemotherapy started. The issue of infection remained the biggest concern with his lung condition and the airway being blocked. Fortunately, his fevers had been improved and I was assured that if a new fever developed, it would relate to a new infection. Regardless of the known complications, I could never have predicted all the new problems that would arise in the next several months.

The first day of chemotherapy actually went better than expected. There was no sign of nausea and his vital signs remained stable. He had 20 days until the next treatment would be given. Would he survive the next 20 days? Would the treatment benefit be enough to justify another treatment at that time? With his condition so precarious, how would I even have enough information to decide? For most cancer treatments, at least two or three cycles of therapy are needed in order to access response. Six to nine weeks seemed like an eternity to wait to find out. Would there be clues to his response?

The first day of chemotherapy treatment going well doesn't mean the rest of the treatment cycle will go so well. At this point one needs to be diligent to watch for signs of infection and issues of bleeding. We did have at that time a newer medication called Neupogen. Neupogen is a bone marrow stimulant to help increase white blood cell production that is generally markedly decreased after chemotherapy administration. With the lowered white blood count, the risk of infection rises drastically. Despite Neupogen being given, his white blood count dropped to very low levels. With continued daily doses, the white blood count recovered. However, Billy had both a staphylococcal infection found in his blood from the central line catheters requiring the line to be changed and antibiotics to be added including Vancomycin and Ceftazadime.

The most confusing issue that developed during the first cycle of chemotherapy was a frothy pink to red fluid from the lung airways that was being suctioned from the tracheal tube. That is the tube that was supplying oxygen to Billy to his lungs from the ventilator. I asked for cultures to be sent on that and luckily no infection was found. Could this material be from the tumor in the airway? If it was the mass in the airways making that fluid, I hoped that was a good sign that the tumor was shrinking. However, his fevers continued and more antibiotics were added including Acyclovir to cover herpetic infections and Flagyl to cover infections of the stomach and intestines, based on the advice of the Infectious Disease service. Having trained at MD Anderson, I knew the use of many types of drugs to treat infections were common place for patients in these situations. As studies have shown over the years, and advances of antibiotics continued, usually patients are on a more streamlined combination of agents to treat infections, today.

Despite all that, I really had little information while approaching the second cycle of chemotherapy. I checked his Chest X-ray for clues. His lung fields were now looking closer to normal. There were no indications for any recent developing pneumonia. There was no evidence of enlarged lymph nodes. I evaluated his left arm area and other lymph nodes sites. I could feel very little in the left armpit and no other lymph nodes were found. That was the best news I could offer. With reservation, I related to Leah that I felt the treatment had helped the lymphoma, but I could offer no real evidence. His oxygen requirement remained unchanged and there was little change in the air way pressure applied by the ventilator to move oxygen into his lungs. A concern for continued oxygen use meant an increased risk of toxicity on the lungs.

Chapter 27 - What Else Can Happen?

November 18: Billy began with his second treatment. Tonda stayed with Billy long enough for me to be able to get back to the apartment for a shower.

November 22: Blood was pooling in the bag coming from Billy's Foley catheter. We are told that Billy's kidneys had begun to shut down. He had to have dialysis three times.

November 22: Tonda and I had frequented the blood bank so often that we became friends with the technicians. We got to know Annetta, Lillian, Evelyn, Lupe, Frank, Joe, and Gerardo. That would make us laugh constantly. What a relief. Gerardo asked if he could give platelets for Billy.

Thanksgiving would be next week. My Mother was visiting at this point and we expected to spend the holiday at the hospital until Gerardo invited us to his house for Thanksgiving. My mother, whom we called Memaw, and I went back to the apartment and watched Andy Griffith and Bewitched. There was something about the innocence of these shows and watching them with my mother that was so comforting, like being cuddled up in a warm blanket.

November 25: Robert and Walter, two of the ICU nurses, spoke about being alert to everything around us and how God can present himself to us at any time. I could feel that God was using everyone around me to give me messages that pointed to His presence.

November 28: The dinner at Gerardo's was so nice. His wife's three brothers, one sister, spouses, and seven children were there. It was the most American Thanksgiving even though everyone was speaking Spanish.

All during this time, cards flooded in, over 400 by December 1 with which I had covered his walls. I am sure this was a fire hazard and totally against policy but no one had the heart to tell me. Strangers began coming to the room door in ICU and asked if they could come in to see Billy. They had heard about Billy and his room from someone and just wanted to see him and be in his room.

This seemed odd that strangers would want to visit someone in ICU but I knew that what was happening here was much bigger than all of us. It was during this time that the larger corner room in ICU became available. The staff approached me about moving Billy to the larger room. He had been there so long that they felt like he deserved it. The average stay for a patient in the ICU would be about 3-5 days and Billy had already been in ICU over 60 days. Tonda told me that she knew it sounded funny but that she was afraid for Billy to leave the room that he was in. She could feel God's presence in His room. I knew exactly what she meant. I could feel it too as I had invited God daily to the room and asked Him to bless all those who came into the room, but I told her that I knew God would move with us.

A fund was started which had over $10,000 in it, $3000 of which was raised from a golf tournament that Jay Tillman organized, "The Billy Benefit Open."

Tanya, one of the nurses, took us to lunch and to the mall one day. It was a relief to get outside for fresh air.

It was during this time that Tonda and I were on the way home one night and the cab driver inquired about why we were at MDA. When he found out that my husband, Billy, was in ICU he asked if he could pray for his brother, Billy. He was from Africa. His prayer was the most powerful prayer that I have ever experienced. His deep voice resonated. In his prayer, he asked for God's healing power to touch Billy's body. Tonda and I got out of the car and stared at each other speechless. We felt as though we had entertained an angel. Who would ever expect to have a spiritual experience in a taxi cab in Houston, Texas?

Chapter 28 - Kidney Failure

November 18 through November 29: The second cycle of chemotherapy using CHOP started on time. That was encouraging considering all the issues we had encountered on the way to making a diagnosis and starting the first treatment. I remained concerned that the second cycle could lead to a complication we couldn't reverse. The second treatment day of CHOP went as well as the first. There were no signs of any distress with the drugs being administered. The neupogen was started again to help with risk of infection. Here was the next waiting game. Give treatment and hope for the best.

The reddish fluid that seemed never ending from the lung airway for the last 3 weeks seemed to taper off. What was changing for the worse were his BUN and Creatinine levels. The Blood Urea Nitrogen level (BUN) and Creatinine are lab values measuring kidney function. The rise of those values meant Billy was rapidly going into acute kidney failure. The Renal Service initiated hemodialysis on November 22. No one knew how many treatments he would need and even worse if the kidney function could improve. The addition of more catheters into the blood to perform dialysis increased his infection risk. Fortunately, Billy only needed three dialysis treatments to lower his kidney function test levels toward normal and balance his electrolytes and reduce the acidosis level his body had during the kidney failure. His levels never rose again.

There was no clear cause of this kidney issue although drugs, overwhelming infections, and tumor lysis syndrome were possible causes. Perhaps it was what we call multifactorial in the medical profession. This means a little bit of all those issues may have contributed. The testing for tumor lysis syndrome, which is a kidney failure process seen from the toxins poured into the blood stream from rapid breakdown of tumor cells, seemed inconclusive. Certainly, he had been on many medications that effect how the kidney can function including the Amphotericin and Vancomycin. I was encouraged that his kidney function returned to normal. The kidneys are very important to clear out the chemotherapy drugs or their metabolized products. While we want the chemotherapy drugs in the body for a period of time to do their work, staying around too long can increase the risk of complications and toxicities.

Chapter 29 - The Calm before the Storm

In the years after Billy's event, I read my journal and realized my entries had totally changed from events and emotions from the onset in September to clinical data and lab numbers in early December. I guess I was unable to keep dealing with the daily emotional drain. I am a banker in my professional life and use numbers all the time. Interest rates had turned into oxygen levels. White blood counts and platelet levels became the interest rate and the amortization. My day became absorbed with studying the vital signs and temperatures, the ventilator settings, and the daily lab values. I talked in terms of tidal volumes and PEEP levels. It was a way for me to objectively measure how Billy was doing and if there was any change in the right direction. It was hard to describe Billy's condition when family and friends would inquire about his status. If you said he was doing better, they might think he was out of the woods when really, he was still unconscious on a ventilator but just not as close to death as the day before.

November 30: Billy's white blood count started dropping.

December 1: When I came in this morning at 5:15 and said, "Hello Billy", he smiled. Elation is an understatement to describe how it felt to see a response from Billy. Vivian was his nurse this day. As I came in she remarked how God is always there and that we must learn to look past the situation to God's promise. As you would expect things have taken on a different perspective.

His fever stayed lower today at 100 degrees but he is still breathing fast because he is acidotic.

September 2 – December 1: There had been many up's and downs from September 2nd to December 1st but for the first time in early December Billy was showing some gradual improvement. During this time, he had lost over 60 pounds and his muscles had completely atrophied. Every weekend when the staff was thinner and doctors less available there would be new crises. I dreaded the weekends. For example, seven days after treatment there would be oxygen de-saturation, severe hemorrhaging, new infections, fevers, and blood pressure and heart rate spikes to dangerous levels. There was no interaction with Billy until early December and I began to wonder how a body could withstand all of the damage that must have occurred with the internal bleeding, blood pressure reaching 250 over 160, heart rate spikes of 180, scarring of the lungs from the pneumonia, dialysis, and chemotherapy. How much can a body repair itself?

During this time, over 60 people have entered ICU with only a handful leaving alive.

Through it all I have had a peace that God has a plan for Billy and that it's not his time yet. God has sent so many angels and signs for comfort.

A CT scan and a bronchoscopy were conducted to see to see if the chemotherapy had been effective.

Two of the 4 chest tubes were removed. The remaining two would be taken out once his platelets topped 75,000.

The X-Rays reflected improvement. Oxygen levels and ventilator settings were lowered toward more normal levels; however, blood gases continued borderline acidotic due to the fevers.

At first, I thought the fevers must be due to the cancer since the blood cultures were negative; however, I learned that, with antibiotics, infections do not always show up.

Our friends call frequently inquiring about Billy's condition. These include David, Val, Kay Maddox, Sarah, Kathy Hairston, Tonda, Lydia, and Brad.

Billy's uncle, David, had two ministers visit Billy who prayed earnestly with him. They placed their hands on him.

My friend from work, Mary Rob, flew down with her husband to be with my Mom and me. They drove us around.

It was amazing to me that people continued to reach out and many to travel 2000 miles to be with us and comfort us.

God has been merciful to Billy and me in the midst of our tragedy.

By now they have refined the diagnosis to, Large-cell aggressive Histiocytic Lymphoma. I heard it presented like Hodgkin's disease but with a cell structure of Non-Hodgkin's Lymphoma.

December 2: It is now the 14th day after the 2nd Chemotherapy treatment. He received 10 more cards today. Although his lab values were improving, his fever stayed at 100 degrees and he was unresponsive today. The pulmonary physicians had been able to lower the pressure on the ventilator enabling them to lessen the sedation so Billy began to interact for the first time in 10 weeks. He could not talk but he started mouthing words. It was comforting to have any interaction with him. The doctors were considering a new trach that would enable Billy to talk. It was exciting to think that after all these months we would be able to communicate to each other again. He was mouthing words but it was very hard to interpret and it was mutually frustrating for both of us as I couldn't understand him. Brennan Kierzek died of Leukemia today. He was only 20 years old. His mother and her sister, younger brother, and father had been staying in ICU around the clock for several days. I watched as the younger brother anguished in pain in the ICU waiting room.

December 3: The kidneys are holding but fevers persisted at 102 degrees. All other lab values were improving. We took brownies to my friends at the blood bank today and saw Liza and Monica. Tomorrow they will take another chest tube out and perform a bronchoscope on Billy.

December 5: Billy's co-workers - Brad and Buzz – flew out to see Billy. Billy was so glad to see Brad. He asked Brad about his job. Of course, this was with motions as he could not speak with the present trach. He was the most awake he had been since we arrived in Houston in September. His platelets were at 81,000. They couldn't start chemotherapy until they are at 100,000. His liver values were elevated but the kidneys were still holding. Dr. Linke talked to Dr. Silmon about Billy going home next week. The doctors back home were anxious to get Billy back to North Carolina.

December 6: Billy asked where his Mother was and if he was going home. He responded so well to Brad. Buzz donated platelets for Billy. Chris from the Blood Bank picked me up at 6:00 and took me to Chili's to meet the crew from the Blood Bank. Gerardo and his wife took me home. They are so precious. They told me a lot about Mexico, their home.

December 7th: Billy's platelets reached 100,000 so chemotherapy would start today!!!! Kidneys were stable and his liver was improving. Gerardo let Mom and I borrow his car. We went to Target, Fiesta, and Red Lobster. We bought Gerardo a poinsettia and wrote a thank you note. Gerardo came by to thank me graciously. I decorated Billy's room for Christmas.

Dr. Peters took Billy's last chest tube out. He asked Billy if it hurt and Billy mouthed, "A little bit". Dr. Peter's asked, "How do you feel?" Billy said, "Fine". Then Billy mouthed "I've got to go to the BATHROOM!

Billy pulled my hand over to him, pulled me down to him and kissed me. Finally, being able to interact with him gave a feeling of normalcy.

December 8: Billy was trying to talk all of the time and was getting frustrated with me. That was ok. I was just glad to have him back. We watched football all day today. Billy's Oilers played the Steelers and won 31-6.

My Mom left. I felt so lonely and really had nothing else to say.

December 9: Billy was talking all day today and was very agitated. He seemed calmer with me in the room and the ICU staff wanted me to stay. However, after staying up most of the last 2 nights I was so tired and wasn't offering much help so I went back to the apartment at 12:15, took 2 Tylenol, ate some crackers, and took a ½ hour nap. Rhonda Phillips called and came by the apartment. Gerardo called to check on Billy and me. Everyone commented on all of Billy's cards.

December 10: Billy was really getting frustrated when I couldn't understand him. I tried to explain to him all that had happened while he was asleep and he said, "I'm not stupid!" He asked about food. He was still on a feeding tube because of the trach to the ventilator so there was no way he could eat. He asked for just a little bit, motioning with his finger and thumb. – "apple and a drink", he mouthed. "Just a Sprite?" Unfortunately, the answer was, "No." We started moving his legs more. His lab values continued to hold at more normal levels.

December 11: Billy has been more patient. I wondered if they gave him more sedatives. He wanted to go to the bathroom really bad...NOT the bed pan. He wants me to stand by the door to keep guard. He had no idea that there is very little privacy in ICU situations. He got a Popsicle today. He was so excited. They sat him on a bed side commode.

I can't believe that I have not written anything about Dr. Linke. She has been a perfect doctor for Billy. She is the one that insisted that they treat Billy aggressively when others were giving up! She is fun and optimistic. She and I talk football all of the time. She knows the division of each league. I know the logos and quarterbacks well.

Before we left Greensboro for Houston, Anne, my friend at work had prayed that God would go before us and prepare a way. He did. He had Billy misdiagnosed to get us to a hospital that would treat Billy aggressively and to a Doctor like Dr. Linke who's not only very competent but a wonderful person too.

Billy got a "communa-trach" and was able to talk for the first time in almost three months. The staff attempted to help him stand. He supported no weight. I looked at Billy and thought how thin and weak he had become from the robust and energetic husband I had taken to the hospital in North Carolina in August. We called his Mom. He said, "Hello Mom". He responded to her with, "That sounds good. That sounds really good. I had better go. I love you."

December 12: He could not sleep at all last night. During this time Billy was more alert and became more agitated. I was trying to rest on two chairs pulled together to form a make-shift bed. It seemed like the night times were his worst moments. He would get very confused and then by the morning he would be more oriented. During the night Billy asked me if we could start going to my brother-in-law, Ken Lyon's, church. He slept from 5:00 until mid-morning. They sat him up twice and he supported none of his own weight. His Physical Therapist said he was much stronger than the previous day. It must be all relative.

They lowered the pressure on the ventilator.

December 13: When I came in this morning, Billy looked over at me, smiled, and opened his arms wide to hug me. He asked me what the next move was and told me he wants to go home for his next treatment. I asked him if he wanted to say anything to Dr. Linke before she left and he said, "Hasta la Vista."

All lab values continue to improve and for the first time there is evidence to support our hope.

December 14: Hope is so fleeting. Friday night Billy was sick all night long. He did not want anyone to suction his trach. He claimed there were drugs under the bed and that they were giving him cocaine. He said that one of the nurses was licking cocaine off of the floor. Every time he would go to sleep someone would wake him to suction his trach, take blood, take blood pressure, etc...

Lydia returned today. It was great to see her. She stayed with Billy Saturday night and gave me a break. Saturday night Lydia and Billy experienced the same thing of continued agitation and confusion. She spent the night trying to re-orient Billy and trying to calm him down. Billy's breathing became faster and faster and his heart rate rose higher and higher.

December 15: Billy's heart rate reached 172 and breaths per minute were in the 50's – twice the norm. I wonder how high it can go before it bursts. He said he was in pain. X-rays revealed no problems and actually revealed some improvement. His sedation was increased.

December 16: Billy was much calmer. His heart rate and breaths per minute were much improved but now his platelets were dangerously low this morning. I asked the nurse to be sure that she asked the doctor for a transfusion of platelets. Dr. Linke called them at 7:00 a.m. and asked for platelet transfusion to be given STAT.

The nurse asked if we had children. I told her about our Dalmatian puppies and that Jazmine was Billy's favorite. Billy motioned me over to him and said that I was his favorite. I felt special.

He asked for his cologne and new pants and when he was going home. Billy has been to the brink of death for 3 months and now he is asking for daily things as if he was admitted for an out-patient surgery.

Billy still had not gotten his transfusion of platelets when at 5:00 p.m. he started profusely bleeding from his trach. The doctors did not know if the bleed was from a superficial wound or deeper in the lungs. Lidocaine was injected into the trach to deaden the cough. Within an hour the bleeding stabilized and decreased through the night. I was sitting in his room and had started writing in my journal when the nurse came in and started to suction out Billy's breathing tube. When she pulled out the suction tube, bright red blood spewed out of the tube and gushed like a geyser and worsened with each attempt to suction. It was coming out of the trach itself. I felt bad that I had left the hospital for a few hours this day, although I knew that I should be able to depend on the medical staff. Lydia and I set out in the hallway outside of ICU hoping and praying that the bleed would stop. We were both in severe anguish on this drastic change of events.

Within the hour, Dr. Linke came to his room. She had been planning to go to a staff Christmas dinner. She was very upset that the platelets which she ordered at 7:00 a.m. had not been given. It would be a shame for him to survive all of his illnesses and then to die of a preventable hemorrhage.

All during this time, I continued to take breaks in the ICU waiting room. Billy's Dad, Bill, was visiting again. He would get the names of people just a little wrong, consistently. Lydia and I would correct him but it did not help. Because we had been here so long, we would answer the Medical ICU waiting room phone with a greeting, "MICU Waiting Room". Sometimes Bill would answer it and he could never get it right. His greetings would alternate between CIA, CLU, and MIA. You could tell from his response that the callers were confused. Earlier in the day Sister Alice brought Billy's dad, Bill, a bouquet of flowers for his birthday. We were in the ICU waiting room. I was sitting at the desk answering the phone. Bill was facing me and Lydia was behind him. Lydia asked Bill who gave him the flowers. He told Lydia that Mother Teresa brought them to him for his birthday. Lydia's face lit up with glee as she worked to keep from laughing out loud.

December 17 – 18: Billy was sedated most of these days. Liza took us to Good Company Seafood, The Galleria, and the grocery store. It was so nice to get outside the hospital walls for a little while and do normal things. We got a report today that Billy's CT scan showed no involvement of the liver and spleen and no enlarged lymph nodes. It was such a relief to know that the Lymphoma had not spread and was showing signs of response to the treatment.

December 19: The bleeding from the trach had not set Billy back too far. The ventilator setting was lowered back to the settings before the bleed.

We went to dinner with Dr. Linke at Kim Som and had some shrimp and noodles. Dr. Linke told us about how she got into the medical profession. On the way back to the hospital, Dr. Linke drove over the curb of the parking lot thinking it was a driveway. Lydia called it Kim Som's cliff. Lydia started to tell Lu the story about a church member who went for a two-day trip and ended up having a triple by-pass. When she turned to Lu she saw Lu shaking with laughter. I am not sure what got them tickled but as Lydia told the horrid story she and Lu laughed harder. Dr. Linke appeared oblivious to them. Thank goodness.

Chapter 30 - What are we saving him for?

I rounded on patients and saw Billy in the early morning and it appeared his temperature was dropping with the change of antibiotics. His platelet count had dropped quite rapidly to 16,000 and I ordered a transfusion of platelets. Billy seemed to be progressing well with the reduction of the ventilator and using the tracheostomy tube instead. He was doing physical therapy to help build up his strength. He remained on total parenteral nutrition, which is the nutritional feedings thru the central line into the vein.

It was the end of the clinic day. I was finishing up notes on patients seen in the clinic and those discussed in our late afternoon case presentations regarding new patients or problem situations. I was sitting in my office hoping to leave soon for a Christmas dinner that I had planned for my staff at Churrasco's. Churrasco's was a fairly new restaurant in Houston known for excellent cuisine from Argentina and surrounding South American countries. I had been there a few times and wanted to share that experience with my staff. A Research Nurse, Judy Howard, was in my office waiting for me to finish up my work so we could drive there together. My beeper rang. I looked at the number and it was the extension to the Intensive Care Unit.

I called ICU and talked to the nurse who was taking care of Billy that day. She related that Billy was bleeding thru the tracheostomy tube. I asked her to explain where the blood was coming from and she stated it just recently started. She wasn't sure if it was the tracheotomy site that was bleeding or further into the lung or airways. She related that the tracheotomy dressing was soaked with blood. I asked if Billy had gotten his platelets that day. She related he had not received them. I asked her to check on the status of platelet transfusion and she voluntarily added his vital signs were stable. I told her I would be right there. She seemed surprised that my arrival would be possible so quickly. I replied that I was in my office and heading that way.

I related to Judy that I would have to go to ICU and she knew it was a situation that was unexpected. She stated she would call to the others arriving to dinner, so they would know they should get seated at the restaurant and start with drinks and appetizers without us. I was already heading down the three flights of stairs to ICU.

As I walked into the ICU, I passed Lydia, Leah's sister, sitting by the door jamb to room 200. Billy had been moved to 200 at some point in his care as it was a slightly larger room. I looked at her eyes and you could tell she was quite concerned with this unexpected development. While she was rarely in the major discussions, I felt she was very reluctant to have this situation with ongoing care continue for Billy. I asked her to make sure everyone was in the waiting room in a few minutes so we could discuss this new problem.

I went into the room and noticed first that his vital signs were anything but stable. His heart rate was up to 140. Normal heart rate is between 60 and 100. His blood pressure was elevated. I was relieved it wasn't low. His breathing was up to 34 times a minute even with the ventilator back in place to help support his breathing. He was back asleep now on sedatives for the evening. What suggested stability to the nurse?

 The respiratory therapist was in the room looking at the dressing of the tracheotomy site and making adjustments on the ventilator. The nurse was standing at her work desk with her back to the patient's bed. I asked the respiratory therapist if he knew where the bleeding was coming from. He was unsure but was getting ready to take off the dressing around the tracheal tube site. I grabbed a pair of gloves and helped him remove the gauze and tracheotomy tube wrappings. The blood appeared to be coming from the airway, as the surgical site was clean and dry. That was not good to see with his lungs being so ill for the last three months. Could the bleeding be from the suctioning they had done in the airways or could it be far worse and be from the lungs itself? Neither sounded that good at the moment.

 I asked the nurse if the platelets were on the way to the room so they could be given. She replied she hadn't had time to check. I looked at the

Respiratory therapist with total desperation. He looked totally confused. I related to the nurse that the platelets needed to get here as quickly as possible and she better be calling Blood Bank to have them sent to the Intensive Care Unit. The nurse left the room.

The respiratory therapist told me he had some ideas on what to give in the airways to help control the bleeding with his breathing treatments. I asked him what he had in mind and he said some lidocaine with the albuterol treatment. This could possibly reduce his cough reflex and help constrict the blood vessels to decrease the bleeding. We finished placing a new dressing on the tracheotomy site and we went to order the breathing treatments. I asked him if he would be here for the evening shift and he related he would be. I told him I would be calling him in about 30 minutes to get an update. I advised him we needed to try to avoid further suctioning unless it was absolutely necessary. I asked for a chest X-ray to see if there was evidence of a bleed in the lungs or a new pneumonia or infection. I hoped that wasn't the case.

I went back to check on the nurse who had arrived from the blood bank with a bag of platelets. I went off to the Intensive Care waiting room. The last two weeks had finally gone smoothly and now this unexpected turn. I had no idea how Leah and the rest of her support group would take this news. Lydia had talked to them already, I was sure. I didn't know until then that she was a Nurse and now they were more concerned than ever. She was certainly aware that this could be a major complication and could relate to a bad outcome. I informed them that I had no idea what was bleeding but it was clearly from the lung itself or the major airway to the lung. I was hopeful this was a superficial bleeding source rather than something deeper in the lungs. I was hopeful the platelet transfusion and the breathing treatments would offer some help to slow it down until the area could heal. I felt that any procedures in this situation would actually increase his bleeding. I related that I had cautious optimism that we could get this to stop with the treatments that we started. I am sure that did little to abate their fears and did little to help mine either. I related that I would be out for the evening but checking in frequently with the nursing and respiratory staff and would be able to come back in, if needed.

I raced back up the stairs to grab my personal items and leave for the restaurant with Judy. Judy decided to drive and we drove to Churrasco's arriving fashionably late. Drinks and appetizers had been served. We ordered dinner and I went to find a phone to call back to Intensive Care. No one had cell phones in those days. The bartender was nice enough to let me use the bar phone.

When I called, I asked for the respiratory therapist. He came to the phone with really good news. The platelets had been transfused as requested and the bleeding had stopped. With little material in the tube, we opted to hold further suctioning through the night. We would do more of the breathing treatments every four hours and reassess in the morning. I could go back to enjoy dinner with my staff feeling confident we were back on the right track. Certainly, it would have been a shame to make all this progress and lose him to bleeding in the lungs.

I arrived the next morning to Billy's room to find no further evidence of bleeding. His platelet count had risen from the transfusion given in the evening to 54,000, which was helpful to prevent further bleeding. Another crisis abated. How many more could Billy handle? How many more could the medical staff handle? The Pulmonary Service decided to wait a few days until his blood counts recovered more to continue the ventilator weaning process. Billy was back asleep again.

December 18, 1991 - December 24: This week was full of the complexity of low blood counts and the risk of infection and bleeding. The bleeding came with the platelet count down again. It resolved with further transfusions of platelets. Fortunately, by the time a week passed his platelet count had recovered back to normal. He was now on four antibiotics and Fluconazole to cover fungal infections. He had a recent blood culture showing a candida infection in his blood. His fevers really did not resolve totally this week.

Cultures of blood and sputum and urine did not show us an infectious source. When blood counts are low in patients receiving chemotherapy, the source of infection could be missed about 50% of the time with testing. Despite that, we empirically start antibiotics to cover infections as their outcome is improved. I had always worried an infection could develop we couldn't control. The central line was changed again. The pulmonary service advised leaving him rest longer on the ventilator with these issues of fevers and lowered blood counts.

On December 19th, I invited Leah and her friends and family that were in Houston to join me for dinner at a local Vietnamese restaurant called Kim Som. In those days, they had converted a ranch house to a restaurant. The food was good, fast and cheap. My favorites were the Spring Rolls with a peanut sauce used for dipping and a rice noodle dish with vegetables, a vinaigrette dressing with grilled chicken. I would usually add a spicy red sauce to the vinaigrette, that my friends and I called Rooster sauce. The bottle that the sauce came in is a clear plastic bottle with an outline of a rooster on it and Oriental style lettering. I would learn many years later from food shows that this is called sriracha sauce. Regardless, it added the right touch of spice to the mixture. I told them about these being my favorite foods on the way to the restaurant. None of the group had ever tried any Vietnamese food choices before. The waiter was quite surprised when we all ordered the same thing, with the exception of Leah, who requested the noodle dish with grilled shrimp instead of the chicken. It felt good to mingle with this group outside of the hospital. I doubt I could have had the strength to do this earlier in Billy's stay at M. D. Anderson Cancer Center.

It was around this time, that I felt Billy had a much-improved chance to make it through all of his health problems. I was sure he would be left with some disability, such as needing oxygen due to the damage he suffered to his lungs. Perhaps he would have a recurrence of the lymphoma and need further therapy, but I felt he could make it home. A Nurse Clinician, Sue, that worked with our group felt less confident that Billy would survive this.

She related to me that it seemed impossible that Billy could survive this with all the issues he had and complications he was getting each treatment cycle. I related that I felt the complications were more in line with a usual cancer patient and felt his lung condition had improved considerably. She felt another bad issue would arise that we wouldn't be able to treat. This was the day of THE BET. I related to her that if Billy made it out of our hospital, even on a ventilator by air ambulance to go to North Carolina with little chance to survive, she owed me a bottle of Dom Perignon Champagne, 1983. I had never tried that champagne, but had heard it was the best modest money could buy at that time. Most places sold one bottle for around 150 dollars. I also related that if Billy didn't survive, I owed her nothing. I related that to this point I had paid with all I had, my knowledge, my continued belief that medicine was doing their best, and my faith that our hard works mattered in his outcome. She accepted that bet to my surprise. My optimism would be short-lived.

As the time neared the holiday break, for which I was getting ready to go home to visit family in

Ohio, Billy persisted with fevers. We were awaiting any information from the blood cultures and testing to see if the antibiotics chosen were correct. These fevers were delaying further chemotherapy treatments. His blood counts were lagging behind in their recovery as well which would hold back further chemotherapy.

Chapter 31 - Letting Go and Giving it to God

As we approached the Christmas holidays I became weary with the overload of information, the day to day routine that never seemed to end, the constant set-backs, and the realization that very few patients had made it out of this ICU. My intent was to journal the daily events but it was increasingly difficult to have anything left to give at the end of the days. My documentation through the end of 1991 was primarily of his labs, vital signs, and ventilator settings.

December 20: Billy was sedated and stable. All counts were improving except for his platelets.

December 21: Lydia left. It was so lonely.

December 22: Billy had a "butt rash" nurse. I was trying to love her but she is frustrating me. She insists upon using the auto-cuff for blood pressure even though it is inaccurate and it is off 30 points. With persistence, she acquiesced. Billy started coughing and some bleeding started. Some bronchitis was present. Sedation was increased once again.

It was a gray day. I became fearful with these events although he had been through much worse. I was so afraid of another set-back. We were so hopeful that Billy would be off of the vent by week end...

Billy was hanging in there although he would smile and weep. I continually prayed for healing, strength, patience, and peace for Billy.

December 24: Billy had a peaceful day. His sedation was lessened again. His lab work showed continued improvement. The ventilator support was lowered some. Tomorrow his sedation would be lowered which would enable the weaning from the ventilator to proceed as long as the platelet count held and there was no reversal in his condition.

The CT Scan showed no lymph node abnormality and he had no fever for the first time in weeks! Praise God. Dr. Linke said there was "marked improvement" but when she saw my excitement she felt the need to clarify that his lung condition was still really bad, but he was responding and there was an improvement!

Today Jane, a special nurse, brought Billy and I a present – a stuffed Dalmatian and scented bath accessories. Phyllis brought us a walking Dalmatian that barks. Gerardo brought us a Texas style bag and bandanas. They are all angels. God is so good. If we have to hurt, God was still blessing us. Liza brought Billy and me a Michael Jordan magazine, Dalmatian book, reindeer necklace, and candy canes.

My family was begging me to come home even if it was only for a couple of days. The thought of leaving Billy even for a couple of days was painful. I did not think I could leave as much as I wanted to see everyone. What if there was an episode? What if he has only days to live? I did not want to miss a minute with him.

December 25: Billy slept all day and asked us to wait until tomorrow to celebrate Christmas.

December 26: A major fever and cough started this morning. Antibiotics were increased and blood cultures taken.

December 27: It was determined that the central line was infected.

December 28: Billy's mother came. I left for Greensboro after the central line was pulled and the fever went down.

When I arrived at the Greensboro Airport there were over 20 people there. At Memaw's, everyone gave Billy and I money for expenses. At home the puppies went crazy. Lou, Lydia, my niece, Jennifer, and I went to the mall. In the hat department, we tried on the wildest hats, especially Jennifer. It felt odd being out of a hospital environment.

December 29: Church at Ken's, my brother-in-law. Josh and Jennifer, my nephew and niece, spent the night with me. We sat up until 2:00 as the dogs lay with us chewing on all their toys. Racquetball with Ken and a movie with Josh and Jennifer followed. We packed in a lot of love and fun. The break was great but I was aching to get back to Billy.

December 30: Tonda and I left for Houston. I was anxious to discover the state of Billy's condition.

When we arrived In ICU Billy has had no fever and was waking up. Lu was obviously so tired from staying with him that I suggested she leave for a while. They had just inserted a new central line which was bleeding profusely. I checked the pillow under his head and it was soaked in blood. The nurse changed the dressing three times and each time the blood soaked through the pillow case. The nurse was so busy that I could not get her assistance and I felt the responsibility for his care and wondering again if this was a superficial bleed or a sever hemorrhage that, while uncommon, could occur with the placement of central lines, and could be fatal. Finally, after four attempts the IV team arrived and was successful in clotting the line. His fever continued to stay down, his platelets held, and his kidneys and liver functions looked good.

December 31: As the year was coming to a close, the ventilator was at its lowest setting and the pulmonary doctors started talking about taking Billy off the ventilator and moving him to a regular room. A CT Scan of the chest was completed and it showed all the lymph nodes in the chest and in the left armpit area were resolved. That was extremely good news.

At 8:30 p.m. Billy started to vomit and convulse for no apparent reason. His blood pressure shot up to 220 over 160. His head thrust back, his arms went stiff out by his side with his hands balled in fists, and his total body went rigid. Tonda and I ran out of the room and down the hallway looking for the medical staff. Thankfully there were several that came running behind Tonda toward me almost immediately. I was so afraid that he was having stroke. Was he to come this far against all odds to succumb to a stroke? Normally I would have stayed with him during these events. If this was it, I didn't want him to be alone, but at this point I had had one too many emergencies. I told myself that I needed to get out of the way because the doctors needed room to work on him but in reality, I could not take anymore. When would it stop?

When the doctors came out to speak with us Lydia asked if the seizure could be withdrawals from high dosage of Morphine that he had been on to keep him sedated for so many weeks. The doctors said that he would not have withdrawals. Lydia said that she couldn't believe he would not have withdrawals because they had administered the Morphine for so long at levels high enough to kill a horse.

I went down to the Chapel to be alone. I asked God that if he was not going to heal Billy's body to please take him now and not allow him to suffer any more. I thought I understood that He intended to heal him but I was ready to accept His will, whatever it would be. I was letting go. It was as if it at this very moment of letting go that there was an immediate turn in this journey. There were to be no new set-backs after this crisis.

Chapter 32 - On the Edge

December 23, 1991 thru January 1, 1992: While I was away in Ohio visiting family, plenty of events occurred to make my optimism for Billy's full recovery less certain. His cultures showed a fungal infection that was now being treated with Fluconazole. The Infectious Disease service decided to avoid Amphotericin which I think in part related to the prior issue of the kidney failure. After a week, it appeared that his fevers started to resolve. With these infections and set-backs, the reduction of the ventilator went more slowly.

Pulmonary Service was continuing now to lower his ventilator support. At times he made good progress, but he did tire out from breathing on his own and needed to have resting periods. The Pulmonary Service was trying to increase his time off the ventilator support and shorten the times of ventilator support. On December 31,1991, Billy suffered from a seizure while still on the ventilator. While it is unclear why the seizure occurred, A CT Scan of the brain showed no major abnormality. Neurology Service suggested watching this situation. Luckily, no further seizures occurred. The reason for that seizure remains elusive but could have related to lowered doses of the sedatives.

As the year closed, Billy started to show progress again in his breathing and Pulmonary Service was continuing to lower his ventilator support. At times he made good progress, but he did tire out from breathing on his own and needed to have resting periods. The Pulmonary Service was trying to increase his time off the ventilator and decrease the time on the ventilator support. For me the waiting game continued until more chemotherapy could be safely administered. A CT Scan of the Chest was completed and it showed all the lymph nodes in the chest and in the left armpit area had resolved. While dichotomous or mixed responses can be seen to cancer treatments, I was hopeful this meant all of the areas of lymphoma were responding. I had already observed reduction of the lymph nodes under the left arm while a mass was growing in the airway. However, all the complications during December caused a delay to starting his next chemotherapy treatment. He was already 2 weeks past the time to start his fourth cycle of chemotherapy, due to infections and a prolonged delay in platelet count recovery. His platelet count that needed to rise to 100,000 had stalled at 60,000.

Without further treatment, the risk of recurrence of the lymphoma would be greatly increased. However, the risk of an untreated infection with chemotherapy would be far worse. Remaining diligent to look for infections and treating them quickly would continue to be a high priority.

Chapter 33 - Real and Sustained Progress

January 1, 1992: Despite the recent events, within a day Billy was almost back to previous vent settings. He was chilling and nauseous but with no fever. Billy asked Dr. Peters to take the NG tube out. Dr. Peters asked, "Oh so now are you going to start telling us what to do now? I don't have time for this." I didn't know Dr. Peter's motivation for being so rude. Perhaps he thought I was telling him what to do as I conveyed Billy's expression of nausea due to the tube and asked about the gastric tube which was an alternative that was discussed. I think Dr. Peter's did not want to do anything that could risk another setback. The NG tube was removed.

January 2: Billy was not as nauseous. The previous evening Billy rubbed my head and hair and asked me to lie down with him. He scooted over for me. I nervously climbed in the side carefully trying not to pull any tubes or set off any alarms. He put his arm around me and told me to relax. The next morning, he laughed at me and said, "You should have seen yourself sleeping last night." Then he scooched up and made fun of me. I loved having this normal interaction!

The Respiratory Therapists (RT) came in periodically to program the ventilator and give Billy breathing treatments. In the process that would unhook Billy from the ventilator, hook a bag to the trach and manually bag him to continue the oxygen flow. Later, when the Respiratory Therapist came in to program the ventilator, Billy took the bag out of his hand and started to bag himself. You should have seen the RT's face. For so many months Billy was unconscious so this is the first they had seen his sense of humor.

The doctor told him that he was breathing mostly on his own. Billy said, "It's only giving me two breaths." – referring to the ventilator. The doctor said, "Thanks Billy for letting me know." Billy said he was scared that the cancer wouldn't slow down. Dr. Linke explained how much he had improved. He started running a slight temperature in the evening. His platelets were still low but starting to rebound. Chemo would probably begin Monday. The ventilator weaning should start tomorrow.

January 3 - January 6: His liver and kidney functions continued to look good but his platelet count had stalled. His temperature was ranging from 99 – 101 so a new antibiotic was started.

January 4th: At 9:45, the trach collar was put on and the respirator was cut off for 3 hours. He tolerated it well. He sat up in a chair for 30 minutes and was in good spirits. We watched football all day.

January 5: The trach collar was placed on at 8:45 and Billy wheeled around the unit outside of his room for the first time in 3 ½ months. He seems a little blue this a.m. because things seem to be moving so slow. Dr. Peters explained that he will stay off the ventilator all day this day, on tonight, off all day and night tomorrow and move to a regular room in 2 to 3 days. We were ready to watch football all day. Funny how doing nothing means so much more.

January 6: The chest x-rays looked great! Emmett Smith met Billy today. He is a social worker. When he left Billy had this sheepish smile and asked, "Who is that, Gomer Pile?"

He had been off of the respirator since 10:10. He was put back on the respirator at 8:00 and asked for a salad. He asked me about his check and commission. He told me, "I would never have been able to make it through all of this without you."

January 7: His platelets were still not rising. A bone marrow test was scheduled for the next day. His spirits were pretty good. He told me that I looked so pretty. He went to physical therapy. Billy did great.

January 8: His platelets rose to 71,000. The bone marrow procedure was done. It was so painful. Several attempts at inserting a new IV were unsuccessful. His veins had collapsed after so many IV's. Afterwards he said he felt like a human pin cushion. Billy's real interested in the "Tonda/Gary" item. He went to physical therapy again. Although I had been telling Billy the date every day, it hit him for the first time today that he had been asleep for 3 months. He thought it was November. He had no memory of anything prior to January 1, 1992.

January 9: Billy threw a pillow at me. Everything was improving but his platelets. So far, his bone marrow looked normal. We met with a discharge nurse to discuss alternative facilities. She said that he would always need to be hooked up to portable ventilator. He would never be able to walk a long distance.

Liza took Tonda and me to lunch. The doctors talked about a subclavian catheter procedure. Billy was afraid. We had devotions and he asked me to say a prayer for him. I assured him that I do all the time.

Billy asked me if he had had chemotherapy yet. I realized that he must not know about the new diagnosis. When I told him the good news that he had Non-Hodgkin's Lymphoma instead of sarcoma he cried. I asked him if he realized that lymphoma was a curable and a more easily treatable form of cancer. He said he had a coach in high school that had it and was told he would be ok and he died three months later. I explained that treatment was much more advanced since then.

January 10: The respirator was moved out of the room today! His bone marrow was normal but his platelets were still not going up probably due to the antibiotic which would be continued for a few more days. We would be moving to a regular room on Monday. Billy asked me if I could move back out of his face a little. I was sucking up all of his oxygen. Billy told me last night that I was the most special person he had ever known.

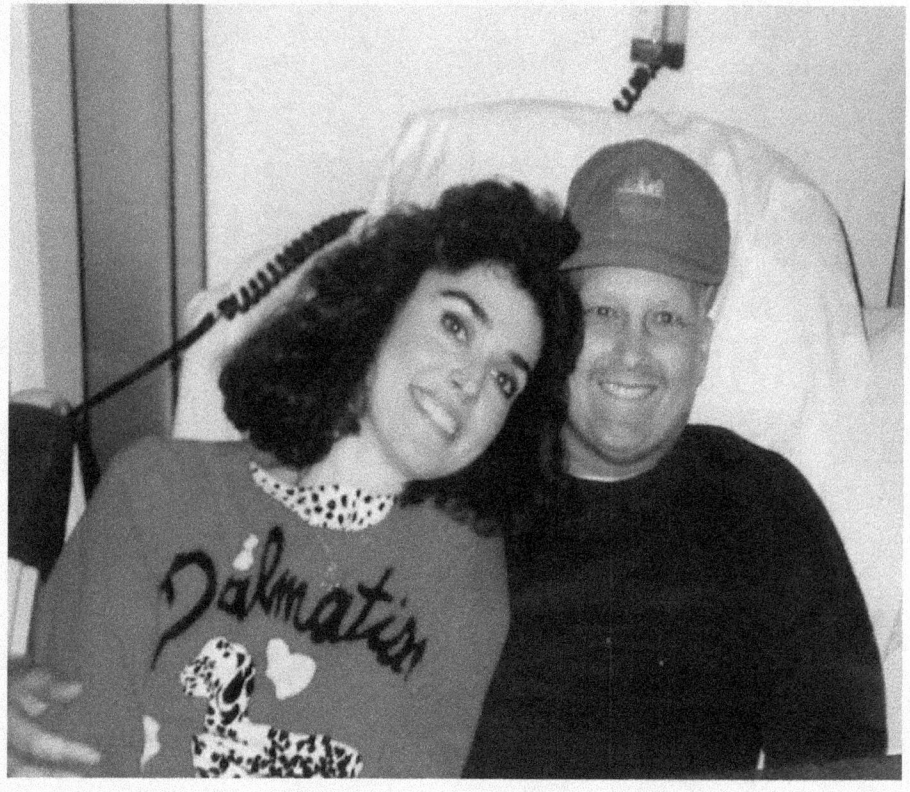

January 13: His platelets rose close to 100,000, the level required for chemo. After two painful

attempts, the dreaded subclavian was performed at 10:00 p.m.

January 14: Billy would probably move to 8024 on Thursday. His 4th round of Chemo was started. The communa-trach was removed and a smaller metal one reinserted.

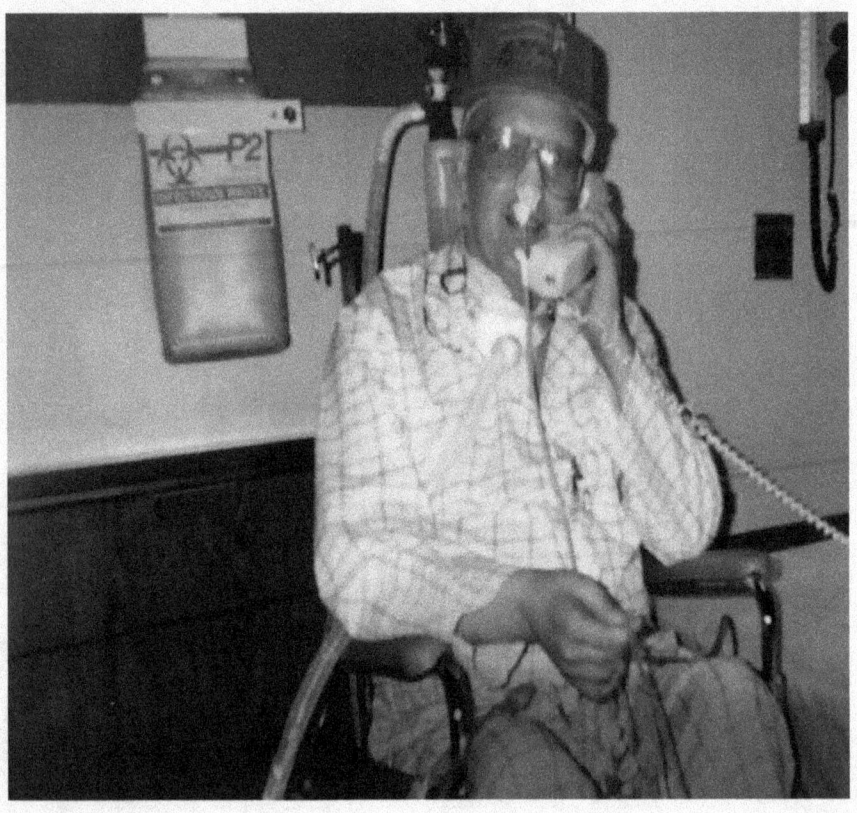

Chapter 34 - Patience

January 1, 1992 thru January 14, 1992

While waiting for an appropriate time to start Billy's next chemotherapy treatment, the first two weeks of the New Year wore on, continuing with the same issues. The blood counts didn't recover to the levels needed for the next chemotherapy. This is when everyone needed a major dose of patience. Guidelines over the years of studying chemotherapy use help set blood count levels that are needed to proceed with the next treatment. With blood counts too low, the risk of complications particularly bleeding and infections rise. If too much chemotherapy is given in a short period of time, one can risk having a bone marrow go into prolonged failure. With his blood counts still low at January 7th, I planned for a bone marrow biopsy evaluation. I needed to know if the bone marrow was still okay and if there were any issues causing the bone marrow to keep blood counts lower than expected. It can also be used to look for some infections that could be present and also to evaluate the lymphoma status in that area. In a few days, the bone marrow report came back that it was still normal. Cultures showed no new infections. His antibiotics and Fluconazole were continued. Despite looking again for causes, nothing new was found. I was left with hoping the treatment given would be enough.

During this time, his weaning process from the ventilator progressed very well and the ventilator was totally removed from the room on January 10, 1992. Close to four months had passed now and his condition while improved still had major issues to resolve. He remained on three antibiotics and the Fluconazole for the fungal infection. He remained weak and his eating had to improve. He was working hard in physical therapy. I was hopeful he could soon be moved out of ICU to a regular hospital room soon.

Chapter 35 - The Parade!

January 16: Billy moved to room 8024! The unit had a parade of balloons, confetti, with the theme song from Rocky playing as he was wheeled down the hallway out of the unit. Billy told Dr. Linke he had a plan. "Pull the trach tomorrow. Pull the nose thing on Monday. Give him a week to see how his intake was after chemo. Give him the once over on Monday and then he is out of here on Tuesday or Wednesday." Dr. Linke asked for an alternative plan. Billy said he would have to get back to her on Plan B.

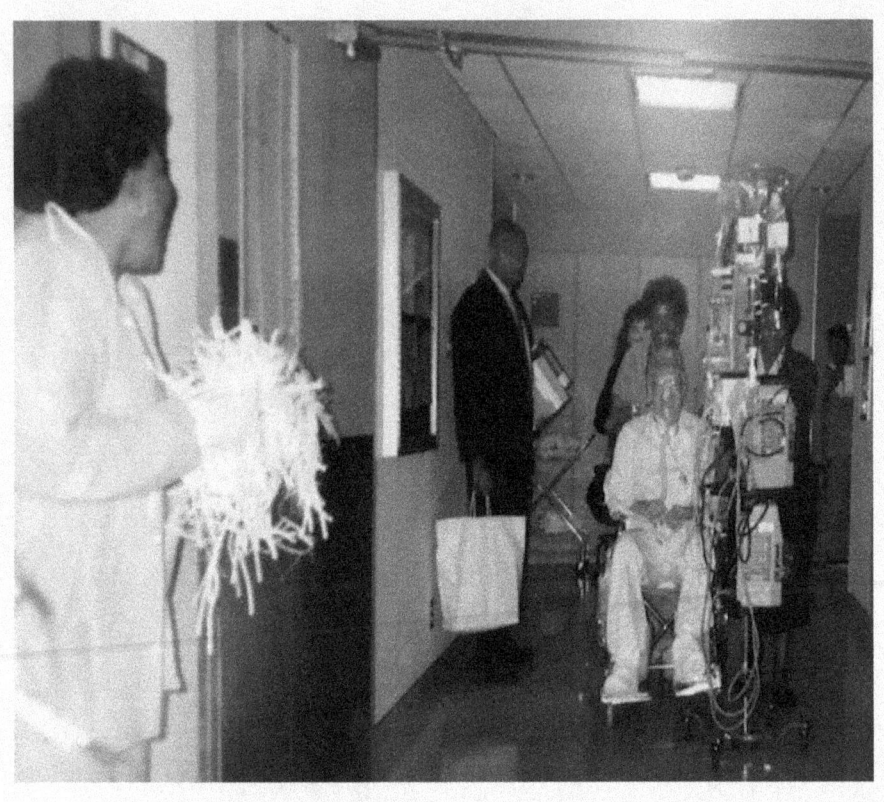

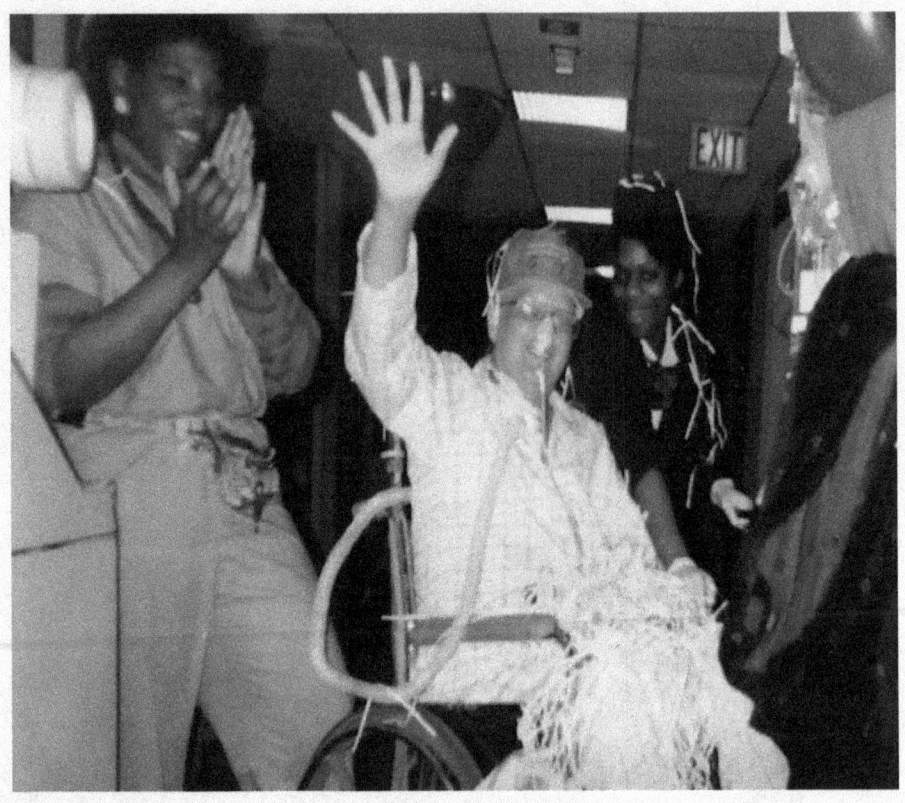

Tonda and I decorated Billy's room with Balloons, streamers, and a plant. Tonda started talking about going home. Billy and I both did not want her to go, but I could not ask her to do any more than she already had. Later that day, Tonda said that she had decided to stay a few more days. She said that when I had stepped out of the room Billy had begged her to not leave and it was impossible to tell him no.

I called everybody to give them Billy's number. Billy slept well.

January 17: His platelets were at 98,000. Brad came back again. Billy was so delighted.

January 18: Billy was eating well!

January 20: His nose tube was taken out.

January 21: It was 7 days after his Chemo so his blood counts began to drop. He took 9 steps on the parallel bars.

January 26: Billy told me yesterday that even though this happened he still considered himself lucky to have me. His temperature rose to 102 degrees so they were checking for infection. The trach was to come out tomorrow barring any complications. His white counts were still extremely low but started up yesterday, 500 from 200. Tonda went home yesterday.

January 27: Billy walked with a walker today. The Trach is out!

January 29th: Moved out of the apartment today.

January 30th: Sue, the nurse clinician, just told me that out of the 12 years that she has worked at MDA, she has never seen anyone recover from as many serious complications as Billy had; that we were a "shot in the arm" to the whole institution.

Billy and I talked about the scripture on hope and how we were forced to live and experience hope which is for what you cannot see and we were forced to wait for God's plan to unfold.

February 1: It was a beautiful day so the nurse unhooked the IV and I wheeled Bill outside for the first time in 4 ½ months.

February 6: We loaded Billy in an ambulance to take him to the airport for the flight home to Greensboro. It was hard to believe we were actually going home. Our friends lined the tarp cheering for us as we deplaned - another parade. We went straight to the hospital.

Chapter 36 - Plan B

January 15, 1992
The long wait for Billy's blood counts to recover so chemotherapy could resume had finally arrived. His Platelet count rose to 101, 000 and his temperature was back down to normal. I chose after much discussion with several doctors to change the chemotherapy. Several new combinations of drugs were showing promise in the treatment of more aggressive types of Non-Hodgkin's Lymphoma and the feeling that changing therapy may decrease the chance of residual lymphoma cells being resistant to the newer treatment. I chose the regimen called MINE. This combined the drugs mesna, Ifosfamide, Novantrone and Etoposide. This treatment was a three-day regimen. Mesna is actually a medication that lowers the risk of bleeding from the urinary bladder lining that is caused by breakdown products from the Ifosfamide. Billy certainly didn't need another site of bleeding.

While setting up for the chemotherapy plans, I related to the nurses in Intensive Care that I felt it was time for Billy to move to a regular medical floor. They felt he should stay. That was quite a change from a time when I was told he was too ill to be in Intensive Care. I stuck to my belief that Billy needed a change in situation so he could feel we believed he could make it. Simultaneously, I discussed with the nurses on the 8th floor that Billy would be coming out of ICU the next day.

The next morning brought great excitement. He was moved from the largest room in Intensive Care to a corner room on the 8th floor. The corner rooms have a much larger space and window views to Holcombe Boulevard. The Intensive Care staff did a great job making his exit memorable. While the nurses played the theme to Rocky, Billy told me he had a plan.
"Pull this tube tomorrow. (He was pointing to the tube in the neck at his tracheotomy site.) Pull this tube on Monday. (He was pointing to the nasogastric tube.) Give me a week with the chemotherapy to see how I am doing. Give me a once over on the next Monday. (He used both hands to motion going over his body.) Send me home on Tuesday." I requested a different plan, knowing one week would not be enough after the chemotherapy to know he was doing okay and typically the week after that was the time he had the most problems with chemotherapy

complications. Billy said he would have to think about a Plan B and would let me know.

At that time, I did start to make calls back to North Carolina. His referring physician had certainly heard Billy was making great progress now and was excited to make plans for his ongoing care upon his arrival back home. I advised that I felt Billy should be taken to a hospital first so that they could watch him and give his next cycle of chemotherapy. I was planning to keep Billy until his next cycle of chemotherapy was ready to start. I reviewed the treatments we had used and the chemotherapy treatment of MINE. I felt confident they could proceed with this back in North Carolina.

The next 3 weeks went better than most could have imagined in September. Billy had the usual complications of fever and needed transfusions of platelets and blood. He was back on antibiotics. But, Billy continued to improve. His oxygen requirement lowered to a nasal prong now and his progress in Physical Therapy was amazing. He went from a patient that couldn't sit up in bed by himself one month ago to walking on his own and riding a bicycle for 30 minutes a day. Even I was amazed at that progress while on chemotherapy. His eating improved and he was starting to put weight back on. Despite the intravenous nutrition he received, Billy had lost a significant amount of weight while in Intensive Care.

Word of his recovery spread throughout the hospital. One day as I stopped by to see Billy, he related that people would come in the room and talk to him. He stated he didn't know who they were. I assured him that it most likely was people wishing him well in his recovery and trying to grab onto some hope for their own situation. It became clear to me that Billy had no idea what he had endured while asleep on a ventilator.

Although slightly behind Billy's plan, Billy was released on a Tuesday, February 6th. He was admitted to his local hospital when he arrived there to start his 5th cycle of chemotherapy with a second cycle of MINE treatment.

As I arrived to work on Wednesday, I unlocked my office door and on my desk sat a bottle of Dom Perignon Champagne, 1983. I wondered what it tasted like. While it signified winning THE BET, it couldn't taste as good as the success we had witnessed over the last 6 months.

For me, the major daily care of Billy Price had

ended. Leah would call to update me on his progress and complications that Billy was having in North Carolina. While Billy had the usual common problems with chemotherapy, he continued to make tremendous strides and was back home. He continued on home physical therapy. At times, I am sure Leah called just to make sure the physicians there were doing what I thought should happen. I knew they were doing the right thing.

All the ups and downs and unexpected twists while caring for Billy Price would be in my past. The 6 months had been totally draining and equally rewarding. While I knew I didn't accomplish this alone, I had been a major force in making sure all involved did what they needed to do. It was not easy convincing other medical professionals at times to follow the lead of someone just 2 months out of Fellowship training.

During the fall, I had taken my Medical Oncology Boards and was waiting for the results of the examination. With little fanfare, I did find out soon after Billy was released to North Carolina that I had passed my Boards. I declined taking the private practice position in Ohio and opted to stay at M.D. Anderson Cancer Center with the Department of Melanoma and Sarcoma. I had completed the sarcoma data base and it was helping us to set useful guidelines on planning therapy for sarcomas.

I had found along the way a confidence in myself to ask more questions, avoid bending to pressure from others, and continue searching for possible solutions. Staying at M.D. Anderson offered to me the ability to try newer treatments in clinical trials with recently found chemotherapy agents and with new combinations of those chemotherapy drugs that showed to help reduce cancers. Newer testing in pathology and radiology would also help to advance out knowledge of cancers, their spread and response to treatment. Newer agents were being developed to alleviate the complications and symptoms of the chemotherapy drugs.

The world of medicine is an ever-changing field and all of us need to keep that moving forward. The advances of medicine over my lifetime alone have shown to increase the survival of most cancers most remarkably over the last several decades. Progress has been made in other areas of medicine as well. Yet, more progress is required.

Chapter 37 - Unusual but Happy Anniversary

February 7: The 5th round of chemo was started. I was so worried about how responsive his NC doctors would be on the 7th day when his counts started dropping.

February 12th: We left for home for the first time since September 17th.

February 14th and February 15th: As hard as I tried to communicate how Billy's condition would deteriorate rapidly on the 7th day we spent the major portion of both days in the ER getting platelets. I even tried calling the blood bank myself to give them a heads up that he would be needing platelets. I guess they didn't honor my medical degree from the Holiday Inn Express. The doctors did not listen to my pleas to schedule a platelet infusion for the 7th day. The doctors NC were not used to patient/family participation.

February 27th: We were in the hospital for Billy's 6th round of chemo and all was going well.

February 28th: It is our 5th wedding anniversary and we were sitting at the hospital when my sisters came rolling in a tray with spaghetti and sparkling grape juice for dinner with candles and everything. God is good.

Chapter 38 - Dom Perignon

September 19, 1992
The summer had ended and the new NFL Football season was underway. Billy Price had been back to work now. His year off from work had ended. His illness in his past, he made plans to visit back in Houston. He looked over the schedule and decided he wanted to see his Houston Oilers play the Kansas City Chiefs. For those that might not recall, Joe Montana had been transferred to the Chiefs. We were all hoping to see Joe Montana play. He didn't play that day due to a wrist injury. Unfortunately, the Houston Oilers lost that game in overtime by a field goal. It didn't dampen the elation of having him in Houston and not in the hospital.

For me, getting to see the reaction to Billy arriving back at M.D. Anderson Cancer Center was amazing. Even those who knew from keeping in touch with Leah and knew that Billy had been doing well, looked at Billy as if they were seeing a ghost. At this time, he had his hair back, the tracheotomy site was closed with a small scar near the Adam's apple, and he walked thru the halls without any problems sporting a nice tan. What a difference a year made. Even those who had openly doubted the process and treatment given knew they had contributed to an incredible outcome.

Sue, the Nurse Clinician who made the bet over his outcome and paid the debt with a bottle of Dom Perignon Champagne invited us to her house. Leah had made a list of people to invite including nurses, respiratory therapists, hospital volunteers, and friends she had made in Houston while there. It was a great time to share in such an accomplishment. People shared their stories of how they connected to Billy and Leah.

I had saved the bottle of Dom Perignon Champagne, 1983 and brought it to this get together. While sitting in the living room telling stories, I brought out the bottle and told Billy of THE BET. I realized Billy had no realization how sick he had been. Billy sat in shock that people could not believe he could recover. I explained there were many times even I didn't believe he would make it, but felt I had to do what I knew might help. We all shared a taste of the champagne to signify the hope the next year would be much better than the last.

No one would know for sure if the treatment was enough for the Non-Hodgkin's Lymphoma. Billy had based on the known data at that time a 25% chance of a long-term remission. While the year had shown great success, the future remained in doubt.

Over the next four years, I would visit Billy and Leah in North Carolina or spend time with them on vacations. We traveled to Lake Tahoe to ski, spent evenings in their living room telling stories, and visited other family members to hear their perspective. It was during that time that I knew Billy had very little recollection of the whole ordeal, even back to before he transferred to Houston. He would sit in awe of the stories we told. He added very little to the story. I asked Billy if he recalled anything from being in Houston. He told us of a dream he had. He relates that he was in a dark parking lot at a mall and near him two gangs were fighting and going around on flying scooters with machine guns. He could see them in the light and he was lying flat by the edge in the dark corners of the lot. A gang fighter flew up to him hovering around him with the gun pointed at him and ready to shoot. At that time, another gang member flew up beside him and said, "Don't shoot Him. He's too sick."

Leah and I had discussed writing this book from the different perspectives we had for several years. Now the story had a title and one that carried a very high significance. Billy had been too sick. He didn't need any help to die. He needed everything we could do to help him survive, against great odds. That is the lesson I have carried with me in my career. Sometimes, we physicians feel compelled to do a therapy and then find us in a treatment that causes some problems we cannot overcome. Even as sick as Billy was, I always tried to be sure we were doing therapy that offered a benefit and questioned if the medications were part of the problems. Certainly, the kidney failure, the lowered blood counts, and the innumerous infections would be examples of complications that would be classified in that category.

More time has gone by now and at the five-year mark, we considered writing the book of Billy's illness and recovery. Was five years enough? Perhaps. Then at ten years, we talked about it again. Was ten years enough? It almost felt right. But now over 20 years have gone by. Billy has health issues with high blood pressure, diabetes mellitus, venous insufficiency in his legs, occasional bouts of cellulitis or infections of the skin, and was diagnosed with Hemochromatosis. Hemochromatosis is a blood disorder where patients absorb too much iron and the iron overload can damage organs such as the liver and the heart. Billy has to do phlebotomies, which is basically taking blood out of the body, like donating blood, to lower his iron levels back to normal. How ironic that instead of needing transfusions, he needs to have blood removed. But in 20 years, there had been no recurrence of the lymphoma and his prior lung damage requires no therapy at this time. He is not on oxygen and does not use breathing treatments of any type.

People who know Billy and Leah when they meet me call me the miracle worker. I usually say that I did what I was taught to do in medicine. I did what the M.D. Anderson Cancer Center Fellowship program taught me to do to treat malignancies. I followed the advice of the physicians there to help guide me through a situation I had never been in before. I needed many consulting physicians to help in his care as well and was fortunate that they carried along with me the willingness to participate to their fullest. The other Staff Physicians in the Melanoma and Sarcoma Section followed my lead. In fact, on many Monday mornings I was met with information about Billy from the recent weekend and it usually ended with, "I wanted to let you know what I did and I hope I did the right thing." They never questioned my direction of care, my motives or choice of therapy, nor advised me to stop treatment. For a Doctor, just months from finishing training, from Doctors that had years to decades of experience more than I, that is quite telling. I am not the miracle worker, **but I let the miracle happen.**

Chapter 39 - Grow Old Along with Me

March – May 1992 – I learned how to put heparin into Billy's central line and give him shots. Tonda moved in with us. She and my mother would take Billy for doctor visits and Chemo treatment. We built a ramp to the side door so we could wheel Billy in and out. I thought Billy would die of a heart attack a couple of times due to some wild rides down that ramp. When I went back to work it was surreal. I had become so accustomed to life and death that it was hard to participate in the mundane of a normal life. When I witnessed someone get upset and complain over a delay in the receipt of their bank statement, I wanted to describe for them what a real emergency was.

In late April when we were waiting to start his last Chemo treatment, his counts were not recovering. When his platelets reached a safe level, he started with an infection and fevers. He had been through so much and so close to the finish line. He had never complained until now when he looked over at me with that bald head and big eyes and said, "I don't like being me." After his last treatment in mid-May, as we lay in bed one night, I could not hear him breathing. I had grown so accustomed to the bells and apparatus in ICU to measure all of his vital signs. I leaned over him to see if I could see his chest moving. He looked up at me startled and asked, "What are you doing"? Suddenly, I became overwhelmed with gratefulness that he was still here with me on this side of eternity. I said, "Billy, I am so glad that you are here" to which he replied, "Thanks. Thanks. Thanks for having me over". He had no idea what he had been through...

August 1992: Almost one year after this ordeal started Billy was back at work part time. They had said that he would always be hooked up a portable ventilator and never walk a mile but thankfully they were not the only ones in control.

25 years later: In recent months as I have heard the song, "Blessings", written by Laura Story, it has caused me to reflect on how the pain of 25 years ago drew me so close to God and provided such clarity in what is truly important. I would never wish that pain and sickness on anyone but I would not trade the glimpses of His glory in the people we met, my friends, and family.

As the song says, "Cause what if your blessings come through raindrops

What if Your healing comes through tears
What if a thousand sleepless nights
Are what it takes to know You're near
And what if trials of this life are Your mercies in disguise."

When we were first married, Billy would say, "Grow old along with me…the best of life is yet to be" … Who knew that 25 years later…I would.

Epilogue – Perspectives

Billy's Perspective

Billy says:

"I was showering on the morning of September 2 of 1991 and found a lump under my left arm. I thought I had pulled a muscle. The lump did not improve. I saw my Doctor on September 5th and he prescribed antibiotics feeling this area was infected. The doctor did feel this lump. The lump did not improve while on the antibiotics. I was admitted to Wesley-Long Hospital and a biopsy was performed on the lump under the left arm on September 12th. The next day, the oncologist who reviewed my case and performed a CT-Scan related the biopsy showed a sarcoma that had already spread to my lungs. Further surgery was not an option. My reaction was, "Isn't this some shit? Doesn't sound like good news to me." I do remember having more fevers that started after the biopsy and I was placed on more antibiotics.

I was referred to a large cancer center in Houston, Texas for further evaluation and possible treatment options. As I arrived into their waiting room, all I knew was I was getting sicker and sicker. I was admitted to MD Anderson Cancer Center that day. On the third night in Houston, I felt something really bad was happening and they rushed me to their Intensive Care Unit. While I don't recall much of the next 6 months, others have their side of the story to tell.

To Treat or Not To Treat

His Mother's Perspective

As Billy, my son, was in the hospital in North Carolina, we found out from the surgeon that his mass under the arm was a sarcoma instead of the infection they had originally suspected. We were told there was no chance at treatment and his survival was as limited as two months. I felt as if my world had totally stopped and was thinking of ways to get totally out of the situation. I felt as if this burden never left my mind or body. However, his local Medical Oncologist advised that help could be found at MD Anderson Cancer in Houston, Texas and I had a glimpse of hope that my son could get treatment. During the time that we were preparing to go to Houston, I was approached by a doctor's wife, who was a nurse, who related to me, "Pray that Billy has lymphoma, as that could be treated." That became my prayer as I was planning to go to Houston with my son, leaving behind my very ill mother, my husband with heart disease, my other son, and my grandchildren. As we boarded the airplane to fly to Houston, there was a thunderstorm. The gentleman sitting next to me was so scared of making the flight and I felt the thunderstorm outside was the least of my concern.

During the first day at MD Anderson, my hope grew that something good was going to advance with the evaluation there. My spirit latched onto the hope for something better to happen than the news of no hope I had during the recent days in North Carolina.

I would spend most of my time that I could in the room with Billy but many times were limited to visiting hours. I would wander around the MD Anderson Complex to get away from the ICU waiting room. I found the library at MD Anderson and in my reading found a statement about cancer. The statement was that all types of cancer have survivors with treatment and that every cancer had at least a 2% chance of remission with therapy. I found tremendous hope from a statement that 2% of all types of cancers are benefitted with treatment and that every type of cancer has known survivors. To you that 2% chance may seem like nothing, but to me that meant everything.

I had been warned about the dangers of a big city like Houston. One night on the way back to our hotel, we were talking about Billy's situation during the cab ride. The cab driver, a large black man from West Africa turned to us at the hotel and offered up a prayer for us and Billy.

One day while staying with Billy, still on the ventilator, a doctor was talking about the possible problem of brain damage. It was the lowest moment of my stay at MD Anderson, as I had felt his surviving was the main concern of all, and had given no thought to his overall condition for the future. Needless to say, as his mother, I wanted everything possible to be done for my son at all points in his care.

Suellen McCrary – High School Classmate - Perspective

Billy was in my graduating high school class, and when we held our 40th reunion, a Facebook page set up for the purpose of contacting classmates. There was a thread about compiling a list of classmates that had died since graduation so they could be honored at our reunion, and I saw where a couple of classmates had listed Billy as one that had passed away.
I replied to the thread that he was fine and living in High Point, and was planning to attend the reunion.
[3]I am almost certain that Billy Price died. I think I went to his funeral.
I will do a search on obits and see what I can find out[2] was one of the replies to my post.
[3]Billy Price is alive and well. I talked to him the other day; he and his wife are good friends of ours:)[2] was my reply.
Billy did attend our reunion. As Mark Twain said, [3]His demise was greatly exaggerated[2].

The thread of the conversation is below:

Joann Sarti Peck I still can't get over Pete Peterson and Billy Price...
Like · Reply · September 19, 2015 at 10:15pm

∧ Hide 14 Replies

Marie Fennell Follo Billy Price is alive and living in High Point.
Like · Reply · September 19, 2015 at 10:48pm

Joann Sarti Peck Marie Fennell Follo, he was living in Texas at one time?
Like · Reply · September 19, 2015 at 10:49pm

Joann Sarti Peck He had battled cancer very young. His Dad told me about it.
Like · Reply · September 19, 2015 at 10:50pm

Marie Fennell Follo Yes, he was sick and in a hospital in Texas. But he recovered and from last I heard he is doing fine. I feel positive Val would have heard if Billy had passed. He is out of town now so I will ask him when he gets back to double check.
Like · Reply · 1 · September 19, 2015 at 10:59pm

Joann Sarti Peck That's so good to know!
Like · Reply · September 19, 2015 at 11:01pm

Laura Kirk i hope i was wrong about him, i was just going by what someone had told me--Leah Price is here in greensboro, a very sweet girl. you might like/want to check with her--ahe is on fb
Like · Reply · September 20, 2015 at 12:11am

Laura Kirk oops----she is on fb
Like · Reply · September 20, 2015 at 12:11am

Suellen Grove McCrary Billy Price is planning to come to the reunion.
Like · Reply · 4 · September 20, 2015 at 9:42am

Joann Sarti Peck 😊😊😊😊😊
Like · Reply · September 20, 2015 at 10:32am

Debbie Richert I am almost certain that Billy Price died. I think I went to his funeral. I will do a search on obits and see what I can find out
Like · Reply · September 22, 2015 at 3:13pm

The Morbidity and Mortality Conference

Our department of Melanoma and Sarcoma had a daily meeting every afternoon at 4 o'clock. After our Monday meeting which covered issues about Melanoma patients and protocol therapies, I went back to my office to finish up plans for my clinic patients. Dr. Robert Benjamin came in and asked if I could present a case for the Morbidity and Mortality Conference. I related that I could and asked when and where this meeting would be. He related it would be the next day at noon. I asked if he thought presenting Billy Price would be okay and from the look on his face I knew that it was what he had in mind. I related that I would be able to get it together.

Morbidity and Mortality Conferences are to be present patient cases that have diagnostic dilemmas, treatment complications, and patients with several health issues that complicate treatment decisions. Billy certainly qualified for this on all levels. Diagnostic Dilemma? Check. Treatment complications? Consistently. Several health issues complicating treatment decisions? Absolutely!

Before I left for the day, I asked my staff to pull Billy's radiology file and bring to the clinic the next morning. I would make a copy of his history and physical on rounds in the morning. I really doubted that I would need his lab or other reports for this conference.

The next day, after finishing the morning clinic, I grabbed the essential x-rays and my copy of his history and physical and set out for the meeting. I presented first and had the CT scans from his evaluation in North Carolina out and ready to use, along with some pertinent chest x-rays that showed his worsening lung condition and then his progression of improvement.

I related that this was a young gentleman that was presented to his doctor with an enlarging mass under the left arm which he found in the shower and was placed on antibiotics. The mass continued to grow and he was admitted to the hospital and a biopsy was done showing a poor differentiated sarcoma. He became febrile and I showed his CT scan showing the lymph nodes in the middle of the chest, the left armpit and along the left collar bone. He also had significant lung infiltrates. I asked if anyone had ideas about his diagnosis and no one replied. I asked if they felt a soft tissue sarcoma could present this way; still, no response from the audience. I went on to say that he came to MDACC for evaluation and treatment being admitted on the day of his consultation. Despite being admitted, placed on antibiotics, and having a bronchoscopy to help with diagnosis, his condition worsened. He required transfer to the Intensive Care Unit and was intubated and placed on a ventilator. His status worsened despite this care and I showed the Chest X-ray that continued to worsen with increased lung infiltrates to what most describe as a "white-out" lung.

I asked again for a possible diagnose.

A physician replied, "What did his autopsy show?"

I related that there was no autopsy done as the patient was still alive. No one else offered any possible causes for his illness.

For years, as a medical student on rounds in the hospital, as an Intern or Resident, and even through Fellowship, we are asked for diagnostic possibilities on rounds and at meetings. It was shocking to think my colleagues, most with many more years of experience couldn't offer any diagnostic possibilities. To this day, I wonder if they felt the diagnosis didn't matter.

I did go on to say that his bronchoscopy showed evidence for Legionnaires Pneumonia. His pneumonia did improve but elevated high airway pressures led to a second bronchoscopy that showed a mass in the airway and on biopsy a diagnosis of Diffuse Large B Cell Lymphoma was made. I related that while on the ventilator, he had been treated with chemotherapy appropriate for that diagnosis and despite several complications, such as kidney failure and low blood counts and infections, he has continued to improve and is presently on a pathway of being weaned off the ventilator.

I thanked them for their time and headed to my seat for the rest of the meeting.

Despite the fact they offered very little for discussion, I do hope that they realized that for myself as a new staff physician recently completing the Fellowship Program, making a diagnosis is extremely important for making a prognosis and what treatment plans would be options for care.

Billy's Best Friend, David Skeels' Perspective

I first met Billy at Greenboro College. He and I were on the basketball team and shared at least one class together. After that year he decided to pursue other options in life and our paths didn't cross again until after I graduated. We reconnected when we played on the same summer league basketball team at the Greensboro YMCA. Billy was a gregarious, witty guy, lots of fun to hang out with and many were drawn to his personality. I was working in Greensboro at the time but living in Burlington and looking to move closer to work. As luck would have it he was looking for a roommate and we moved into The Glen, a new apartment complex in Greensboro. We did a lot of the things that young single people our age did while living there, parties, going to bars and socializing with friends. The apartment pool was a focal point of social life during the summers and Billy quickly became the unofficial mayor of The Glen. We still found time to play basketball at the Y, usually on Saturday mornings. The basketball courts were located close to the racquetball courts and if you were waiting for the next game, everyone who was going to play racquetball had to walk past us to get to the courts. One Saturday a very attractive young lady with brown hair and big brown eyes caught our attention as she made her way to courts. It goes without saying that we noticed her. Later that night after I had come home from a date and Billy had come home for the evening his first words to me were "Guess who I met tonight? The lady we saw at the YMCA today!" As you may have guessed that young lady was Leah. They dated briefly but for whatever reason it didn't work out at that time. Sometime after that Billy and I moved to a different apartment complex called Yester Oaks. This was an older complex but the apartments were bigger and there were a lot of people who lived there that were our age. The apartments were bigger so we added another roommate, Val who had gone to high school with Billy. He was the opposite of Billy in personality. (Sometimes I thought he lived vicariously through Billy.) At some point during our time at Yester Oaks Billy and Leah's paths crossed again. This time it was serious and it wasn't hard to see this was going to work out this time. Billy was traveling a lot during this time and I got to go out with Leah and her girlfriends. Sometimes it would be six young ladies and me. I wasn't complaining! ☺ The running joke was that I dated all of her girlfriends but that was an exaggeration. Although I could see I was getting ready to lose my roommate of eight years I did gain a good friend in Leah. Billy and Leah got married and moved in to a townhouse and although our lives moved forward we all remained very close friends. A few years later I took a job going to work with my brother who had started a company in the legal tech field. This required that I move to Raleigh. Although I did not see Billy and Leah as much as I used to we stayed in touch and I would come back to Greensboro and see them as often as I could.

I had been in Raleigh about a year when Leah told me that Billy was sick. He was going to the hospital in Greensboro so the doctors could figure out what was going on with him. When Leah called and told me that the doctors had diagnosed him with a rare form of cancer that no one had seen in North Carolina I felt an avalanche of emotions. How could this happen to my friend? They had just gotten married! Why is this happening? On a personal note it was difficult living in another town and not being able to help out as often as I would like or just drop by and see him whenever I could. And now to find out he will be in Texas which seemed so far away. Although I knew he needed to go wherever he had the best chance to get help it was very frustrating to feel like there was little I could do but pray. I wondered how Leah would be able to handle this.

I had a chance to see Billy and Leah before they left and the one thing that stands out in my memory was how big his eyes looked. Not sure what that meant but I can still see that in my mind's eye to this day. I called frequently the first few days he was in Texas and on the second or third day Leah told me if I wanted to say good-bye

I need to come out sooner rather than later. He had taken a turn for the worse and was now on a trach and in a coma. My brother gave me time off to go and on three occasions I would fly out on a Thursday and come back on a Monday or Tuesday. Billy was in a coma for about four months so during my visits he didn't consciously know that I was there. I would talk to him and I would read him stories from the USA today Sports page. Once I thought he opened his

There are a number of memories that have come back to me about those times.

I'm going to recount some of those in a "stream of consciousness format"...

Finding hope in the numbers:

We were allowed four 30 minutes visits daily to see Billy in the ICU every day. We lived for these opportunities to see him every day. He had various machines/devices connected to him each measuring a different value that indicated something important. (Memory escapes me what they meant now.) I remember the first thing Billy's dad would do each visit was check those numbers. He knew which numbers were good if they were high and which ones were good if they were low. The first time I saw him do that I thought to myself "why is he obsessing over those numbers?" I quickly found myself doing the same thing and realized that Billy's dad had figured out that when we saw positive feedback then we had hope that he would beat this. Hope in the numbers.

Sleep:

A lot of the folks who had a family member or friend in the ICU would sleep in the waiting room. The chairs would lay back and the staff would bring blankets and a pillow for each of us to use. There must have 30-40 chairs in there and they were all full. Billy's mom was a prodigious snorer. When she would get going you could see folk's heads popping up all around the room. The times that I was there and she was also there I would give her chair a gentle kick to wake her up and then pretend to be asleep. I sure she knew it was me but I never owned up to it.

Platelet donation – a way to help:

Once they started treating Billy with chemo he needed platelet donations to get his platelet count back up. On my second and thirds visits I was able to donate platelets for him. It is different than a blood donation in that they take blood out, extract the platelets, and then put the blood back in you. It was a relatively painless process but time consuming. It took several hours to do but it made me feel like I was doing something to help him. I don't think I ever told Leah this but on one occasion I had taken a product with aspirin in it and I found out you are not allowed to donate for two days if you take aspirin or something with aspirin in it. I extended my trip an extra day which enable me to donate.

Finding humor in dark times:

It may seem inappropriate to some given the circumstances but when I think back about those times there are a couple of funny stories that have stayed with me over the years that made us laugh at the time. Our friend Val had come out one weekend when I was in Houston and he and I shared a hotel room. Val had a very lean build, the definition of an ectomorph body type, almost cadaverous in appearance. The first night we were taking a van to our hotel from the hospital. Val sat in the very back and I sat up front with the gentleman driving the cab. In a very deep, distinguished baritone voice, he took one look at Val and said to me "Is that the patient?" Val didn't particularly find it funny but I laughed out loud.

There are a number of stories that I heard from Leah about things that Billy did or said after he came out of his coma. After having a trach in his throat for 4 months with his only sustenance a liquid that came from a bag attached to a pole beside your bed, I think Billy was ready for some real food. On one of Dr. Linke's visits Billy was so convincing to her that he had eaten a sandwich, even though with a trach it was physically impossible, to prove that it was okay for him to have some food that she called the nurse in to the room to ask her. The conversation went something like this, Dr. Linke: "Billy says he has eaten a sandwich today." Nurse: "Billy's lying!"

There are hundreds of stories and memories about Billy's illness and subsequent recovery that I could tell you. But this is Leah and Billy's story and she can tell it better than I can. There is one thing I do want to say and I'm sure Billy would agree 100 percent. Billy would not be alive today without Leah. For someone who was young, newly married and short on life experiences to take control of this and battle to keep him alive and get well every day is truly amazing. I don't know many people who could have gone through what she did. Her faith and strength is inspiring.

www.ingramcontent.com/pod-product-compliance
Lightning Source LLC
Chambersburg PA
CBHW051752040426
42446CB00007B/325